antipasti

Fabulous Appetizers and Small Plates

by Joyce Goldstein

Wine Recommendations by Jeffrey Meisel

Photographs by Paolo Nobile

CHRONICLE BOOKS

SAN FRANCISCO

Library of Congress Cataloging-in-Publication Data available.

ISBN 0-8118-4872-8

Manufactured in China.

Designed by **Vanessa Dina**
Food stylist: **Marco Melissari**
Props stylist: **Federica Bianco di San Secondo**
Typesetting by **Janis Reed**

The photographer wishes to thank the following for their contributions to the book: ABITO QUI; Milan, Italy; Tel +39 02 290025184 ::
ARMANI CASA; Milan, Italy; Tel +39 02 723181; www.armanicasa.it :: ARMANI CASA; New York, NY; Tel (212) 3341249 :: BORMIOLI ROCCO &
FIGLIO S.P.A.; Fidenza, Italy; Tel +39 0524 5111, www.bormiolirocco.com :: BORMIOLI ROCCO GLASS CO. INC.; New York, NY; Tel (212) 7190606 ::
CHRISTIANE PERROCHON; Capannole, Italy; Tel +39 055 9910320; www.christianeperrochon.com :: GIUSEPPINA BARANGIOLA; Lurate Caccivio,
Italy; Tel +39 031492404 :: LA CHIAVE DI VOLTA; Milan, Italy; Tel +39 02 8356252 :: MACELLERIA MASSERONI; Milan, Italy; Tel +39 02 89403774 ::
RINA MENARDI; Gruaro, Italy; Tel +39 0421 280681 :: SAMBONET; Orfengo, Italy; Tel +39 0321 879731; www.sambonet.com :: SAMBONET Inc.;
Elizabeth, NJ; Tel (908) 3514800 :: SILVA; Milan, Italy; Tel +39 02 89400788 :: TESSUTI MIMMA GINI; Milan, Italy; Tel +39 02 89400722 :: VINICIO
ZACCHETTI :: Milan, Italy; Tel +39 02 8357020

Distributed in Canada by Raincoast Books
9050 Shaughnessy Street
Vancouver, British Columbia V6P 6E5

10 9 8 7 6 5 4 3 2 1

Chronicle Books LLC
85 Second Street
San Francisco, California 94105

www.chroniclebooks.com

Dedication

For my grandchildren, Elena, Adam, and Antonio.

Acknowledgments

MILLE GRAZIE to:

Bill LeBlond for saying it was time to revisit antipasti and for his loving support of my work.

Sharon Silva, the editing goddess, the best in the business, who pushes for accuracy in many languages.

Jeff Meisel for his wine expertise, excellent palate, and passion for Italy.

Vanessa Dina, a superb designer, and Paolo Nobile, whose photographs are enticing and look good enough to eat. It was a pleasure to be working with you again. You make beautiful books.

Food stylist Marco Melissari and prop stylist Federica Bianco di San Secondo. You make the dishes look as appealing as they taste.

Jan Hughes and Doug Ogan, managing editors with eagle eyes, who proofread and catch all the little errors.

Janis Reed for typesetting and Tera Killip, production manager, who makes sure the printing of the book is perfect.

Amy Treadwell, bravo for organizing all of us!

Gary Woo for testing recipes and tasting food with me for over twenty years. Long may this continue.

Paul Ferrari and Carlo Lavuri, for arranging visits to fabulous food purveyors.

Slow Food and the Salone del Gusto for the opportunity to taste Italy's best artisanal food products.

Dave, Bill, Bob, Pat, Phyllis, and Mark, an intrepid band of traveling companions, you get the awards for enthusiastic eating.

My family, who once again stepped up to the table and cleaned their plates.

Table of Contents

Farinaci

Grains

65

Crocchetti di riso Rice Croquettes 66, Crocchetti di riso al tartufo nero Truffled Rice Croquettes
from Umbria 70, Polenta fritta con crema di formaggio Fried Polenta with Cheese Spread 72,
Pizza di granturco Crisp Polenta Cake 75, Insalata di riso Rice Salad 77,
Insalata di farro al profumo dell'orto Wheat Salad with Garden Vegetables 80

Verdure

Vegetables

83

Carciofi sott'olio Preserved Artichokes 84, Involtini di melanzane Stuffed Eggplant Rolls 86,
Caponata Sicilian Sweet-and-Sour Eggplant 89, Peperonata con patate Sweet Pepper and Potato Stew
from Tuscany 90, Insalata di peperoni verdi Green Pepper Salad 91, Funghi marinati Marinated Mushrooms 93,
Insalata tiepida di funghi Warm Mushroom Salad 94, Insalata di campo con bruciatini di prosciutto Salad of
Field Greens with Crunchy Prosciutto 95, I ripieni Stuffed Vegetables 96, Funghi ripieni al forno Baked Stuffed
Mushrooms 100, Pomodori farciti al formaggio squaquarone e basilico Tomatoes Filled with Creamy Cheese
and Basil 101, Fagiolini alle nocciole Green Beans with Hazelnuts 103, Asparagi al forno e fonduta Roasted
Asparagus and Creamy Cheese Sauce 105, Sformato di cavolfiore Cauliflower Pudding 106

Pesce e frutti di mare

Fish and Shellfish

109

Insalata di mare Seafood Salad 110, Insalata di frutti di mare, arancie e finocchio Shellfish Salad with Oranges and Fennel 113, Insalata di aragosta al pesto Lobster Salad with Pesto 115, Insalata di calamari e carciofi Squid and Artichoke Salad 118, Gamberi alla crema di piselli Shrimp with Pea Purée 121, Scampi al pompelmo Shrimp with Grapefruit 122, Insalata di fagioli e gamberi White Bean Salad with Shrimp 124, Involtini di gamberi rossi in umido di ceci Prosciutto-Wrapped Shrimp with Warm Chickpea Salad 126, Cipollata di tonno Tuna in a Sweet-and-Sour Onion Marinade 127, Capesante alla fonduta di cipollotti novelli e tartufi neri Scallops with Spring Onion Purée and Black Truffles 128, Insalata di capesante e funghi porcini Warm Salad of Scallops and Porcini 130, Sarde a beccaficcu Sicilian Stuffed Sardines 131, Calamari ripieni Stuffed Squid 132, Baccalà mantecato Whipped Salt Cod Spread 134, Cozze al forno Baked Mussels 136, Tartine di patate con pesce affumicato e caviale Potato Cakes with Smoked Fish and Caviar 139, Insalata di polpo e patate Octopus and Potato Salad 140

Introduction

In 1987, I was asked to organize an antipasto luncheon for the first Mediterranean Food Conference, which was to be held in New York. The American Institute of Wine and Food was the event sponsor, and chefs and winemakers from all over the Mediterranean had been invited. As coordinating chef, I contacted American chefs specializing in Italian food and asked them to prepare a signature dish for this prestigious lunch, which was to take place at the then Parker Meridien Hotel. The hotel was to provide a few antipasti, but the main plates were to come from this country's culinary stars.

On the day of the event, chef Todd English, who then headed up the kitchen at Michela's in Cambridge, had to cancel because of a family emergency, and restaurateur Michela Larsen came and executed his dish, an exquisite stuffed calamari. Evan Kleiman of Caffè Angeli in Los Angeles prepared her wonderful eggplant *rollatini* stuffed with fresh mozzarella. I served an updated version of *carne salata,* spiced, cured beef fillet seared rare and accompanied with sliced artichokes and shaved Parmigiano-Reggiano cheese. The opening chef of Manhattan's Union Square Café, Ali Barker, served his contemporary interpretation of *vitello tonnato*. Instead of covering braised veal with tuna sauce, he seared fresh tuna fillet and served it with the classic tuna mayonnaise. To our great surprise, some of the visiting Italians were outraged by the *carne salata* and *tonno tonnato* and staged a walkout at the lunch. Rare tuna! Almost raw meat! They claimed they could become sick from eating these barely cooked items.

But why the melodrama? *Pesce crudo* (raw fish) is a preparation of long standing in the Italian south. Carpaccio (raw beef fillet) has been served at Harry's Bar in Venice since the fifties, and *carne cruda* (chopped raw veal) is a classic of Piedmontese cuisine. So our dishes were hardly radical; in fact, they were based on tradition. The presentations, however, were contemporary, and the Italians were offended at the so-called liberties we upstart chefs had taken with their antipasti. After a few hours of uproar, *Atlantic Monthly* editor Corby Kummer solicited a public apology from the Italians to the American chefs and the meeting continued without controversy.

We've come a long way since those days. Over the past twenty years, an antipasto revolution has taken place. It is not that the traditional antipasti have gone away. Instead, the menu category has been expanded to include dishes that previously have not been considered part of this opening course. If the same conference were held today, there would be no walkouts, and the Italian guest chefs would be serving dishes far more radical than anything the American chefs presented in the mid-eighties.

Antipasto Today

Major lifestyle changes have occurred in Italy since the idyllic time that I lived there many years ago. Except for tourists and a few wealthy Italians who have few time constraints, the long, leisurely lunch hour has vanished, along with the beloved siesta. Women are no longer staying home full-time, managing the household and cooking all the meals. Most people are working longer hours and dining out more often, or relying on prepared foods from the local *gastronomia* or *tavola calda.* Given time and money constraints, they usually do not go out for expensive multicourse meals except, perhaps, on special occasions. Instead, dining has become more casual. With the growing number of *osterie, tavole calde,* simple *enoteche,* and more elaborate wine bars with expanded food service, Italians can spend less—and taste more. While antipasto is still an opening course on the formal menu, dining on an assortment of antipasti, with small plates as the meal, has become a new way to eat in Italy today.

In early Roman times, the antipasto course was variously known as *antecoena,* before the *cena* or "meal," and *gustatio* or *gustum.* The latter terms are related to the verb *gustare,* meaning "to enjoy" or "to relish." In Puglia today, this course is sometimes called *apristomaco,* or "stomach opener." Some Italians refer to these dishes as *stuzzichini,* from *stuzzicare,* "to pick," as in *stuzzicadenti* or "toothpick," while others dub them *assaggi,* or "little tastes." In Venice, they are called *cicchetti.*

In the recent past, only one or two simple plates might be served in an Italian home before the main meal. The elaborate antipasto assortment was primarily a restaurant experience. Today, serving assorted antipasti at home is surprisingly practical. Many dishes are relatively simple to assemble and can be prepared in advance. They can be supplemented by items purchased at a *salumeria, tavola calda,* or *gastronomia* for satisfying shop-and-serve antipasti.

Antipasto is celebrated in both *la cucina classica* and *la cucina creativa.* In the former, the antipasto table offers a stunning array of colorful platters of room-temperature dishes. (During the Renaissance, this array was called *servizio di credenza,* after the name of the sideboard on which the platters were displayed.) Included in the selection are marinated and grilled vegetables, seafood assortments, and sliced meats, augmented by one or two warm last-minute items, all designed to whet the appetite and enhance the dining experience. Local and seasonal ingredients are showcased and traditional recipes are followed. Many chefs who serve *la cucina classica* are inspired by Italy's growing Slow Food movement and its support of time-honored regional foods.

In the contemporary *cucina creativa,* the concept of antipasto has been expanded. The quiet revolution started in the mid-seventies and early eighties, when Italian chefs began to explore the foods beyond their regions. Following in the vanguard of such *alta cucina* chefs as Gualtiero Marchesi, Valentino Marcattilii, and Angelo Paracucchi, many of whom did a culinary stage in France, today's Italian chefs are inspired by travel, work abroad, international food publications, and television cooking shows. They no longer feel that every dish they serve must be tied to a traditional preparation. They will even use ingredients that are not typically Italian, serving foie gras, smoked salmon, gravlax, and ceviche alongside local artisanal products. Many of their recipes are easily handled by the home cook: ingredients are generally widely available, most of the techniques are simple, and relatively few dishes require last-minute preparation.

On the whole, contemporary antipasto presentation has become more elegant. Instead of rustic family-style platters, many dishes are now carefully arranged and served on individual plates. Some are composed salads. Antipasti that traditionally were served at room temperature may now be served warm. For example, what used to be a platter of room-temperature chickpeas topped with cooked shrimp and dressed with a basic vinaigrette is now a warm chickpea ragout with sautéed prosciutto-wrapped shrimp and a rose-mary vinaigrette, all artfully arranged. A warm salad of sautéed porcini atop lettuces is no longer a *contorno,* or side dish. It is instead listed among the antipasti on a menu. Dishes such as a *sformato* (custard) of celery, cauliflower, or cheese, surrounded by a creamy tomato sauce or red pepper ragout, might have been considered a *primo*, or first course, in the past, but now appears with the antipasti as well.

Antipasto Styles

Varied styles of antipasto service are possible. The one you choose depends on the number of guests and your culinary scenario. Will a buffet assortment of antipasti be the meal itself? Or, will you be serving an antipasto before a multi-course meal? Are you planning for an intimate group or for a crowd? Are you serving family or close friends informally, or are you entertaining guests who are not everyday diners in your home? Each situation suggests a different style of service.

For a large crowd, an assortment of antipasto dishes on the buffet table, the classic *servizio di credenza,* is ideal. Offering mostly room-temperature dishes and letting people help themselves will simplify presentation. Most of us do not have the luxury of servers to pass hot offerings, so it is wise to restrict the hot dishes to no more than two or three and pass them yourself (or have a friend or partner help you) or keep them warm on a hot tray. In a more casual setting, you can pass family-style platters of room-temperature antipasti at the table and then serve a few hot dishes as they come off the stove.

Individually composed plates, sometimes served in addition to a room-temperature assortment, work best if the guest list is small. Such plates are usually last-minute creations, most easily served to an intimate group already seated at the table and best suited to formal meals.

In this book, portion sizes are approximate, with the number of servings each recipe yields determined primarily by how many other dishes you are serving. Obviously, the more antipasti you offer, the more portions you will realize from each recipe. (In any case, you won't regret having leftovers.) There is no rule, however, that says you must offer an assortment of dishes as an antipasto course. In fact, one perfect jewel before the meal will suffice to whet the appetite. It might be a fabulous first course in a meal that does not follow the traditional Italian format of antipasto, *primo piatto, secondo piatto, contorno,* and *dolce,* or it might not even be an Italian meal. What is important is that the dish harmonize with the balance of the menu, such as serving an elegantly composed seafood salad to open a formal dinner or a bowl of caponata to begin a rustic supper.

If you are an experienced and well-organized cook, you will enjoy yourself in the kitchen. Preparing antipasti does not demand the gravitas required when putting together a serious formal dinner. None of the dishes is difficult to prepare, although a few may take some time and effort. If you are new to entertaining and a relative novice at the stove, do not worry. Many items in Shop-and-Serve Antipasti will make you look like a professional. You can cook one or two simple dishes and buy a few. Decide on your style of service—casual, formal, or somewhere in between—and then settle on the number of courses that will suit both the style and the amount of time you have to devote to preparation.

Do not get carried away and overwhelm your guests with too much food. Dining should be a satisfying, sensual experience, not an endurance test. In other words, be selective. On almost every occasion, a few well-prepared dishes are a wiser choice than a large selection of fair, hastily assembled plates.

If you are a relaxed cook, last-minute preparations and finishing touches will not worry you, and composing pretty salad plates will be creative fun, not torture. If you are an anxious cook, practice the dishes on your family or best friends until you feel confident to attempt them for a group, or skip the fancy plates in favor of simple platters. If you are pressed for time, put together an assortment from Shop-and-Serve Antipasti and maybe take the time to prepare one hot item. For ease of service, make some of the dishes well ahead of time and have them ready in the refrigerator, so that all you need to do is bring them to room temperature or warm them.

For any antipasto party, you need to select some antipasti that can be fully prepared well ahead of time and keep the last-minute preparations and *antipasti caldi* (hot dishes that are fried or sautéed at the last minute) to a minimum. I won't tell you what dishes to select, however, as tastes are highly personal. But keep in mind that fresh, seasonal foods will always win out over out-of-season extravagances, and that you want a good balance of meat, seafood, vegetables, cheese, and bread-based items or grains. Remember to have enough meat-free and seafood dishes for guests who are vegetarians or eat fish and shellfish but not meat. Offer bread, bread sticks, olives, a bowl for olive pits and used toothpicks, and plenty of wineglasses, small plates and napkins, and knives and forks, if needed.

Each recipe in this book includes a wine recommendation, and most of them illustrate the sound practice of pairing regional dishes with wines from the same area. For example, a dish of briny seafood from Campania calls for a Fiano di Avellino or a

Falanghina, Tuscan liver crostini are perfectly matched with the local Chianti, or a truffled onion-and-cheese *sformato* from Piedmont is complemented by a glass of Barbera d'Alba. Of course, this formula fails if you are serving a large assortment of antipasti from all over Italy. In that case, offer your favorite sparkling wine, a dry, crisp white, and a medium-bodied red, along with water and other beverages.

Finally, no matter what style of serve you choose, always remember to take time to enjoy your own party.

Shop-and-Serve Antipasti

I love to cook. One of my favorite ways to entertain is to serve an abundant and varied assortment of antipasti. On occasion, however, I find myself short on cooking time when I have guests coming for drinks or dinner. That's when the ideas included here come to my rescue.

Entertaining is easy when you know how to shop and how to assemble interesting antipasti quickly. With one trip to the supermarket and/or the Italian delicatessen, I can fill a table with a delicious array of classic and contemporary dishes, and not spend much time, if any, at the stove. I might have to turn on the broiler, toaster oven, or microwave oven briefly, but that's hardly a daunting task.

Among my choices are plates of smoked fish and raw fish, sliced cured meats (*salumi*), and traditional fruit and meat combinations, such as prosciutto and melon, mango, or figs, or *bresaola* with grapefruit. I can serve prosciutto-wrapped bread sticks, or *rollatini* of salami or mortadella filled with herbed cheese. I can offer platters of assorted cheeses and purchased cheese spreads or cheese *torte* (layered cheese terrines), or I can spread condiments like olive purée or artichoke purée on crostini. In my pantry, I always have canned beans and excellent olive oil–packed tuna and anchovies on hand, as well as sun-dried tomatoes and preserved and marinated vegetables. With a few drops of extra-virgin olive oil or olive oils scented with citrus or herbs, a lemon wedge, a few capers, or olives, I can transform the simplest antipasti into platters of *abbondanza* and elegance.

What follows is a list of suggestions for wonderful shop-and-serve antipasti. There are no detailed recipes, but rather thumbnail descriptions that will let you assemble these ideas with ease.

Vegetables

You may have jars of *sott'olio* (preserved in oil) or *sott'aceto* (pickled) vegetables that you have prepared yourself (page 84) already in your pantry. If not, you can buy them. The selection of vegetables packed in olive oil, vegetable spreads, and condiments at Italian markets and supermarkets is amazingly varied: preserved artichokes, roasted peppers, eggplant, or mushrooms; spreads made from these vegetables; various olive purées; sun dried tomato spreads; and products made from combinations of these ingredients. You can serve them with slices cut from a rustic loaf or spread them on crostini, bruschette, or simple toasts.

Another major convenience is the supermarket salad bar, where you can buy precut vegetables. You can serve them in the following ways:

Pinzimonio – Assemble a platter of carrot and celery sticks and fennel and pepper strips, or place vegetables in a clear-glass bowl with an inch or two of ice water. Accompany with extra-virgin olive oil for dipping and coarse sea salt for sprinkling.

Condiglione – To prepare this Ligurian dish, toss together sliced tomatoes, peppers, cucumbers, and onions; chopped fresh basil; and slivered anchovy fillets with olive oil and a tiny bit of vinegar and top the mix with wedges of hard-boiled eggs, if you have them. And if you do not, remember that they take only 9 minutes to cook, so you can boil them while you assemble the vegetables.

Bagna Cauda – This is a tiny cheat because you do have to go to the stove, but you will be there only for a few minutes to make this fast, easy version of the classic Piedmontese dish. In a small saucepan, combine ½ cup extra-virgin olive oil; 6 cloves garlic, finely chopped; and 10 to 12 olive oil–packed anchovy fillets, very finely chopped. Warm the mixture gently over low heat until the anchovies melt. (If you have time, do as the Piedmontese do and simmer over very low heat for about 30 minutes while you assemble other dishes.) Add 4 tablespoons unsalted butter and, when it melts, pour the mixture into a fondue pot or chafing dish and place over a warming candle. If the flavor is too strong for you, add a little heavy cream or whole milk. Serve with an assortment of raw vegetables or strips of coarse country bread for dipping.

You can also offer platters of vegetables:

Drizzle sliced tomatoes and fresh mozzarella cheese with basil-infused olive oil or with a vinaigrette made by thinning prepared pesto with extra-virgin olive oil and vinegar. Or, drizzle with plain extra-virgin olive oil and add a scattering of torn basil leaves.

Toss cherry tomatoes and *bocconcini* (small fresh mozzarella balls) with chopped fresh oregano, minced garlic, red pepper flakes, freshly ground black pepper, and extra-virgin olive oil.

Top sliced roasted peppers and fresh mozzarella cheese with torn fresh basil leaves or rinsed capers and drizzle with extra-virgin olive oil.

Drizzle sliced roasted peppers, slivers of Fontina cheese, and arugula with extra-virgin olive oil.

Top sliced roasted peppers with rinsed capers, olive oil–packed anchovy fillets, and chopped fresh flat-leaf parsley and drizzle with extra-virgin olive oil.

Stuff roasted peppers with herbed ricotta or goat cheese or cheese *torta* and drizzle with extra-virgin olive oil.

Stuff roasted peppers with a mixture of 2 cans (6 ounces each) olive oil–packed tuna, drained and flaked; 2 tablespoons rinsed capers; 3 table-spoons coarsely chopped pitted green or black olives or olive purée; ¼ cup chopped red or white onion; and about ¼ cup mayonnaise to bind. (You can even buy vacuum-packed packages of cherry peppers stuffed with tuna and anchovies.)

Top thinly sliced raw mushrooms and fennel and strips of prosciutto (optional) with shaved Parmesan cheese and drizzle with extra-virgin olive oil.

Stuff celery with Gorgonzola cheese mixed with a bit of unsalted butter and chopped toasted walnuts or hazelnuts.

Stuff Belgian endive leaves with Gorgonzola cheese mixed with mascarpone or ricotta cheese and a few nuts.

Top sliced fennel and carrots with toasted walnuts or almonds and dress with Gorgonzola cheese puréed with a bit of cream or with a drizzle of orange-infused olive oil.

Top radicchio leaves, either torn or left whole if small, and orange segments with toasted walnuts and shaved Parmesan and drizzle with extra-virgin olive oil or orange-infused olive oil.

Combine shelled and peeled young, tender fava beans, diced pecorino cheese, and freshly ground black pepper and drizzle with extra-virgin olive oil. (Preparing this dish can be a great icebreaker or group activity. Put some friends to work helping you peel the favas while you all sip wine. In unity there is speed.)

Combine shelled and peeled young, tender fava beans, narrow strips of prosciutto, extra-virgin olive oil, fresh lemon juice, freshly ground black pepper, and shaved Parmesan cheese; toss well and arrange on a platter. In a pinch, use shelled *edamame* (soybeans) in place of the favas; they are sold fresh or frozen.

Pick up some good-quality olives at one of the many "olive bars" in supermarkets these days and customize them with the addition of thin strips of lemon or orange zest or a sprinkle of red pepper flakes. Also, warming even the most pedestrian olives will heighten their flavor. Put them in a small sauté pan and toss over low heat for a few minutes, or warm for 40 to 60 seconds in a microwave oven.

Cheeses

Drizzle chunks of Parmesan cheese with aged balsamic vinegar or truffle oil. Use only the best here, which means Parmigiano-Reggiano cheese and *aceto balsamico tradizionale*.

Set out wedges of Fontina, provolone, *toma, pecorino fresco,* or others with a loaf of coarse country bread.

Set out creamy cheeses such as fresh *robiola* or goat cheese, firm cheeses such as pecorino or an aged goat cheese, or a blue such as Gorgonzola *dolcelatte* with *mostarda di frutta* (spicy fruit preserve).

Spread fresh *robiola* or goat cheese on crostini or slices of coarse country bread.

Toss *bocconcini* (small fresh mozzarella balls) with extra-virgin olive oil, chopped olive oil–packed anchovy fillets, and red pepper flakes.

Here are some simple warm cheese dishes:

Spoon whole-milk ricotta cheese into a sieve placed over a bowl and let drain for 1 hour in the refrigerator. Spoon into oiled ovenproof custard cups or a small, round baking dish, drizzle with extra-virgin olive oil, and broil briefly or put in a microwave oven for 1 to 2 minutes to warm. Serve with toasted bread or bread sticks.

Mix together 1 pound whole-milk ricotta cheese, 2 eggs, 1/4 cup grated Parmesan cheese, 1/4 cup olive purée, 2 teaspoons dried oregano, and salt and freshly ground black pepper to taste. Spoon the cheese mixture into an oiled small, round baking dish, and put in a microwave oven for 1 to 2 minutes to warm, or bake in a 300°F oven for 12 to 15 minutes to warm. Serve with good bread.

Slice *scamorza*, smoked mozzarella, or *pecorino sardo* cheese into 1-inch-thick slices, brush on both sides with extra-virgin olive oil, and place over a very hot charcoal fire or on a very hot stove-top grill pan or nonstick sauté pan until the cheese just starts to melt, 1 to 2 minutes on each side. Serve the cheese atop grilled or toasted bread for a typical antipasto from Abruzzo. Or, place the cheese slices on an oiled flameproof platter, melt under the broiler, and serve from the hot platter with care. You can top the warm cheese with some chopped sun-dried tomatoes and a bit of chopped fresh basil or thyme or dried oregano. Serve with toasted bread.

Known as *frico*, it takes longer to talk about this simple crisp from Friuli than it does to make it. Preheat the oven to 425°F. Place heaping tablespoons of grated Montasio or Parmesan cheese 1 inch apart on a baking sheet. Flatten them into disks about 2 inches in diameter. Bake the disks until the cheese is melted and golden, 8 to 10 minutes. Using a thin metal spatula, transfer the cheese wafers to wire racks. They will crisp up as they cool. (You can also cook these wafers on a stove-top griddle.) Store in an airtight container for up to 5 days.

Meat and Poultry

Cured Meats (*Salumi*)

Along with a simple platter of sliced prosciutto, salami, *bresaola* (dried salted beef from the Valtellina), and mortadella, you can embellish the slices with a simple twist or roll:

Wrap prosciutto around bread sticks.

Wrap prosciutto around strips of provolone or fresh mozzarella cheese.

Wrap prosciutto around slices of melon, fig, peach, mango, Fuyu persimmon, or pear.

Cut figs in half, wrap in prosciutto with a mint leaf, brush lightly with extra-virgin olive oil, and grill or broil until the prosciutto is slightly crispy at the edges. Best served hot or warm, but if time is critical, serve at room temperature.

Wrap pancetta around figs and broil or grill.

Wrap prosciutto around crisp-cooked asparagus spears and serve warm or at room temperature with grated Parmesan and a drizzle of extra-virgin olive oil.

Roll salami around herbed goat or cream cheese.

Roll mortadella around strips of provolone with or without a smear of mustard.

Wrap *bresaola* slices around ricotta or fresh *robiola* cheese mixed with chopped arugula and drizzle with extra-virgin olive oil.

Assemble *bresaola* slices and grapefruit segments on a bed of arugula and drizzle with extra-virgin olive oil.

Assemble *bresaola* slices and shaved Parmesan cheese on a bed of arugula and drizzle with extra-virgin olive oil.

Assemble *bresaola* slices and artichoke hearts, sprinkle with minced shallots, and drizzle with extra-virgin olive oil.

Carpaccio

Place thin slices of raw beef or veal fillet between sheets of oiled parchment paper or plastic wrap, gently pound until nearly paper-thin, remove the top sheet, invert the bottom sheet onto a plate (or a bed of arugula or other vegetable), peel it away, leaving the meat, and finish as follows:

Make a bed of shaved fennel or thinly sliced raw mushrooms and top with the carpaccio, or top the carpaccio with the fennel or mushrooms and dress both the meat and the vegetables with extra-virgin olive oil and salt.

Make a bed of arugula, top with the carpaccio, top the meat with shaved Parmesan cheese, and drizzle with extra-virgin olive oil.

Make a bed of radicchio leaves, cut into narrow strips; top with the carpaccio, dress with balsamic vinegar and extra-virgin olive oil, and crown with a scattering of toasted pine nuts and shaved Parmesan cheese.

Dress carpaccio with mayonnaise thinned with Worcestershire sauce and fresh lemon juice and a bit of milk to make it spoonable. Or, put mayonnaise mixture in a plastic squeeze bottle and squeeze out a design on the meat. A caper garnish is optional.

Top carpaccio with slivers of celery, escarole dressed with extra-virgin olive oil and lemon juice, and a garnish of chopped black truffle (from chef Gualtiero Marchesi).

Carne Cruda

In Piedmont, hand-chopped raw beef or veal from the prized local breed, *Razza Piemontese,* is traditionally topped with an abundance of shaved white truffle. You may not always have truffles, but you can always serve the beef. For each pound of chopped lean veal or beef fillet, add 2 to 4 cloves garlic, finely minced; the juice of 1 or 2 lemons; and 6 to 8 tablespoons extra-virgin olive oil and mix to distribute the ingredients evenly. Or, season simply with salt, freshly ground black pepper, and extra-virgin olive oil. Serve as is, or top with a bit of truffle oil. For a more dramatic and formal presentation, serve the chopped meat mounded in individual spoons arranged on a platter.

Chicken

Buy a rotisserie-cooked chicken at your market, remove the skin, and then remove the meat from the bones. Discard the skin and bones. Prepare in one of the following ways:

Tear the meat into strips and toss with arugula or radicchio and a small handful of toasted pine nuts. Dress with a balsamic vinaigrette or a good mayonnaise.

Tear the meat into strips and combine with raisins and chopped candied citron, toss with a balsamic vinaigrette, and serve on a bed of lettuce (from Ristorante Il Sole di Maleo, outside Milan).

Thinly slice the meat, combine it with raisins and toasted pine nuts, dress with a balsamic vinaigrette, and serve with celery slices and arugula (from Ristorante Battivacco in Milan).

Tear the meat into bite-sized pieces; toss with 2 fennel bulbs, chopped, and 1 cup toasted almonds and dress with mayonnaise thinned with fresh lemon juice. (Some cooks add slivers of *groviera* or Gruyère cheese or cooked ham.) Serve atop a bed of lettuce and sprinkle with a little chopped fresh flat-leaf parsley or fennel leaves.

Fish and Shellfish

Smoked Fish

Combine softened cream cheese or mascarpone with prepared horseradish and freshly ground black pepper and roll up about 2 teaspoons of the cheese mixture in each slice of smoked salmon. Arrange rolls, seam side down, on a platter and skewer with toothpicks for easy retrieval, or serve on toasted bread. Or, place on individual plates, top with a lemon vinaigrette made with or without mustard, sprinkle with salt and freshly ground black pepper, top with chopped fresh chives, and serve with knives and forks.

Wrap smoked salmon around crisp-cooked asparagus spears and dress with mayonnaise lightened with whipped cream and optional caviar (from San Domenico di Imola restaurant, in the province of Bologna).

Arrange smoked salmon or smoked trout fillets and sliced cucumber or fennel on a platter and dress with crème fraîche flavored with a little prepared horseradish.

Arrange smoked trout, sturgeon, or sablefish; sliced fennel; and orange segments on a platter and dress with a citrus vinaigrette or with orange-infused olive oil.

Arrange smoked trout, sliced boiled potatoes, and diced tomatoes on a platter, dress with a citrus vinaigrette, and sprinkle with minced fresh chives.

Arrange smoked salmon and sliced leftover boiled potatoes on a platter, top with slivered white or red onion, dress with extra-virgin olive oil, and top with plenty of freshly ground black pepper.

Bottarga
Shave *bottarga* (dried mullet or tuna roe) on a salad of sliced tomatoes and cucumbers and thinly sliced white or red onions.

Tuna
Purchase high-quality canned tuna packed in olive oil and prepare in one of the following ways:

Combine tuna, canned white beans, and chopped green or red onions and dress with a lemon juice or vinegar vinaigrette.

Combine tuna, canned chickpeas, diced tomatoes (in season), and green onions; dress with extra-virgin olive oil; and sprinkle with freshly ground black pepper.

Anchovies
Purchase high-quality anchovy fillets packed in olive oil or *boquerones* (Spanish marinated white anchovies) and prepare in one of the following ways:

Arrange anchovy fillets on a bed of sliced fennel or celery with orange segments or toasted almonds (optional).

Arrange anchovy fillets on a bed of sliced tomatoes and onions or sliced roasted peppers.

Layer anchovy fillets on bruschette alone or over roasted pepper strips.

Shellfish
Toss crabmeat with extra-virgin olive oil and fresh lemon juice and garnish with cherry tomatoes or fennel slices or serve on bruschette.

Combine crabmeat, chopped celery, and chopped fresh chives and bind with lemon mayonnaise; serve on crostini, if desired.

Toss shrimp with extra-virgin olive oil, fresh lemon juice, and chopped fresh basil; serve on bruschette or crostini, if desired.

Combine shrimp with chopped fresh basil, bind with mayonnaise, and serve on crostini or use to make *tramezzini* (sandwiches; see page 25).

Raw Fish
Most diners mistakenly believe that Italian raw fish dishes are a contemporary innovation. Serving raw fish, or *pesce crudo*, is an old tradition in Italy, especially among seafaring people in Sicily, Puglia, Liguria, and Campania. In the past, such dishes were not as prominent as they

Antipasti Introduction

are now, but with an active food press and the increased internationalization of cuisine, fish carpaccio and fish tartare have proliferated on restaurant and home menus. Chefs love them because they are versatile and easy. The most important thing to remember is always to use impeccably fresh fish and shellfish, such as tuna, halibut, salmon, and scallops.

For fish carpaccio, gently pound a thin slice of raw fish between sheets of oiled parchment paper or plastic wrap until nearly paper-thin, remove the top sheet, invert the bottom sheet onto a plate, peel it away, leaving the fish, and then garnish. For *pesce crudo,* cut the fish into thin slices but do not pound. For fish tartare, cut the fish in tiny uniform dice and mix with mayonnaise or oil and aromatics. The sliced or diced fish can be briefly marinated, "cooking" it much like ceviche, or dressed at the last minute.

Top raw fish slices with shaved radishes or a fine dice of sweet red onion and drizzle with extra-virgin olive oil and with fresh lemon or orange juice, or a combination, if desired.

Drizzle raw fish slices with a lemon vinaigrette and top with chopped green onions or slivered red onion and with red pepper flakes, if desired.

Combine raw fish slices with grapefruit or orange segments on a platter, drizzle with extra-virgin olive oil or lemon- or orange-infused olive oil, and sprinkle with freshly ground black pepper or red pepper flakes.

Combine raw fish slices with thinly sliced fennel on a platter, drizzle with fresh lemon juice or orange juice and extra-virgin olive oil, and garnish with blanched finely cut lemon or orange zest strips.

Top raw fish slices with chopped tomato, shredded fresh mint leaves, and lemon slivers and drizzle with fresh lemon juice and extra-virgin olive oil.

Dress thin raw salmon slices with crushed pink, green, and white peppercorns; extra-virgin olive and walnut oil; and fresh lemon juice and marinate for 10 to 15 minutes. Serve with a salad of sliced cucumbers dressed with heavy cream thinned with a combination of olive and walnut oils and flavored with fresh lemon juice and minced shallots (from chef Valentino Marcattilii).

Combine 1 pound sea bass fillet, cut into tiny dice; $1/4$ cup mayonnaise, preferably homemade; 2 olive oil–packed anchovy fillets, finely minced; 2 small cornichons, minced; 2 capers, rinsed and minced; 1 tablespoon Worcestershire sauce; 4 or 5 drops Tabasco sauce; 1 tablespoon brandy; and some chopped fresh flat-leaf parsley. Season with salt and freshly ground black pepper and serve with 8 thin slices white toast (from Ristorante Bastianelli al Molo in Fiumicino).

Combine finely diced salmon or tuna, finely minced shallot, extra-virgin olive oil, grated lemon or orange zest, chopped fresh dill, and salt.

Crostini and Bruschette

Crostini are small, thin slices of toasted bread. Bruschette, in contrast, are thicker slices of chewy country bread that are toasted or grilled, brushed with extra-virgin olive oil while still hot, and then, if desired, rubbed with the cut side of a split garlic clove. You can also use pieces of store-bought focaccia, warmed or crisped a bit in a toaster oven.

First, some commonsense advice about toppings: Do not serve bruschette or crostini topped with foods that will tumble off easily when the slice is picked up. There is nothing more embarrassing to a host than to see a guest pick up a bruschetta topped with chopped tomatoes and watch the tomatoes slide onto a shirt, lap, or Armani silk necktie. If you like the look of chunky toppings, serve the bruschetta on a plate with a knife and fork, or top the chopped component with melted cheese to hold it in place, or make a sandwich.

Suggested Toppings

Combine 1 can (6 ounces) olive oil–packed tuna, drained, and 6 tablespoons unsalted butter, at room temperature, in a food processor and process until smooth. Season with a little fresh lemon juice, salt, and freshly ground black pepper, and top with rinsed capers and minced fresh flat-leaf parsley.

Combine 2 parts Gorgonzola cheese and 1 part unsalted butter, both at room temperature, in a food processor and process until smooth. Fold in chopped toasted walnuts or hazelnuts. Top with a thin slice of ripe pear or fig, if desired, or with chopped fennel or celery.

Combine fresh goat cheese with chopped walnuts and chopped fresh thyme.

Combine ricotta cheese with chopped arugula; top with strips of roasted pepper.

Spread with herbed goat cheese and melt briefly under the broiler or warm in a toaster oven.

Smoked mozzarella cheese, roasted pepper strips, and chopped fresh basil; melt under the broiler, if desired.

Combine 2 cups canned white beans, ½ cup extra-virgin olive oil, and 2 or 3 cloves garlic, chopped, in a food processor and process until smooth; season with salt and freshly ground black pepper. Top with diced salami; with canned tuna and chopped arugula; with chopped arugula and black olives; or with anchovy fillets and slivered red onion (the last for bruschette only).

Mashed canned chickpeas; top with chopped arugula or salami, drizzle with extra-virgin olive oil, and garnish with slivered red onion (for bruschette only).

Mashed canned chickpeas; top with chopped shrimp or anchovies, drizzle with extra-virgin olive oil and fresh lemon juice, and garnish with slivered red onion (for bruschette only).

Toss lightly mashed canned chickpeas with chopped tomatoes and chopped fresh rosemary (for bruschette only).

Chopped black olives seasoned with cayenne pepper (optional); top with sliced fresh mozzarella cheese and melt under the broiler (for bruschette only).

Toss together very finely chopped tomato and minced fresh basil (for bruschette only).

Toss together very finely chopped tomato and finely chopped black olives or rinsed capers (for bruschette only).

Chopped tomatoes or sun-dried tomato spread; top with sliced fresh mozzarella cheese and melt under the broiler (for bruschette only).

Mashed artichoke hearts or prepared artichoke spread; top with chopped fresh flat-leaf parsley and rinsed capers or chopped black olives (for bruschette only).

Toss together baby shrimp, chopped arugula, fresh lemon juice, and extra-virgin olive oil.

Sliced smoked salmon, chive cream cheese, and rinsed capers.

Unsalted butter, sliced smoked salmon, and minced fresh chives.

Toss together chopped hard-boiled eggs, chopped olive oil–packed anchovy fillets, rinsed capers or chopped black olives, and extra-virgin olive oil.

Quartered fresh figs and prosciutto slices; drizzle with extra-virgin olive oil and sprinkle with freshly ground black pepper (for bruschette only).

Tramezzini

These small sandwiches are made with white bread with the crusts removed. A slice of bread is spread or topped with a filling, capped with a second slice, and then cut on the diagonal into triangles or, more rarely, cut into fingers or squares.

Suggested Fillings

Smoked trout fillets, cucumber slices, and cream cheese, herbed cream cheese, or cream cheese flavored with horseradish.

Sliced prosciutto, *bresaola* (salt-dried beef from Valtellina), or salami; arugula or fresh fig or pear slices (optional); and unsalted butter.

Sliced prosciutto, chopped *mostarda di frutta* (spicy fruit preserve), and unsalted butter.

Sliced hard-boiled eggs, mayonnaise, and arugula.

Sliced hard-boiled eggs, chopped black olives and rinsed capers, mayonnaise, and watercress or arugula (optional).

Shrimp, mayonnaise, and watercress.

Bread Salads

Use day-old country bread (it should be firm, not soft), remove the crusts, and cut into 1-inch cubes.

Dress the bread cubes with extra-virgin olive oil and some good red wine vinegar, adding just enough to moisten the bread so that it absorbs the oil and vinegar but does not get too mushy or soggy. Let sit for an hour while you set the table and assemble the other food. Then toss the soaked bread with diced tomato, diced cucumber, finely minced red onion, and shredded fresh basil leaves and season with salt and freshly ground black pepper. Add more olive oil and vinegar as needed. Serve at room temperature.

Toss together the bread cubes, bite-sized pieces of cooked chicken, toasted pine nuts or almonds, plumped raisins or currants or fresh grapes, chopped fresh mint or flat-leaf parsley (optional), extra-virgin olive oil, and balsamic vinegar. Warm slightly in a microwave oven for about 30 seconds or serve at room temperature.

Toss together 1-inch bread cubes, shrimp, diced tomato, chopped olive oil–packed anchovy fillets, chopped fresh basil or mint, extra-virgin olive oil, and fresh lemon juice. Serve at room temperature.

Uova e formaggi
Eggs and Cheese

The versatility of eggs and cheese makes them standard fare on the antipasto table. With a little time at the stove, eggs are easily transformed into deviled eggs, frittatas, and rolled omelets, or blended with cheese for warm *sformati* (custards). Eggs and cheese combine beautifully with a bit of flour to become crunchy fritters, and also fill crisp fried zucchini blossoms with their creamy richness.

Uova ripiene Stuffed Eggs

8 eggs

For the tuna filling

3 ounces olive oil–packed canned tuna, mashed

3 tablespoons mayonnaise

1 tablespoon chopped fresh flat-leaf parsley

1 tablespoon capers, rinsed and chopped

1 tablespoon black olive purée (optional)

For the anchovy filling

3 tablespoons mayonnaise

1 tablespoon minced olive oil–packed anchovy fillets

1 tablespoon capers, rinsed and minced

3 tablespoons finely chopped celery or red onion

These eggs are so simple to make they could almost be in Shop-and-Serve Antipasti, except that you have to cook the eggs . . . perfectly. Stuffed eggs are always a welcome addition to an antipasto assortment for two reasons: they can be prepared ahead of time and everyone seems to love them. Be sure to make enough, as they will vanish from the platter rapidly.

I have provided two fillings here, the first made with tuna and the second, for salt lovers, with anchovies. If you do not want to take the time—or have the time—to stuff the eggs, you can instead chop them coarsely, mix them with chopped capers, olives, anchovies, and finely minced celery or onion, or with tuna in place of the anchovies, and spread the mixture on bruschette, crostini, or between slices of white bread as a filling for *tramezzini* (page 25). You can even use it as a filling for tomatoes (hollow them out as directed on page 96, but omit the baking).

○ ○ ○

To hard-boil the eggs, in a small saucepan, combine the eggs with cold water to cover. Place over medium-high heat, bring to a boil, reduce the heat to low, and simmer gently for exactly 11 minutes. (While 9 minutes is my ideal for a hard-boiled egg to eat out of hand—the timing yields a creamy center to the yolk—here you need the extra 2 minutes for the yolk to firm up and become dry enough to mash easily.) Drain the eggs and place under running cold water until cold.

Peel the eggs and cut in half lengthwise. Scoop out the yolks into a bowl and set the whites, hollow side up, on a tray. Mash the yolks with a fork.

Select either the tuna or the anchovy filling, and add all the ingredients for the filling to the mashed yolks, mixing well. Spoon the mixture into the egg-white halves, dividing it evenly and mounding it attractively. Cover and refrigerate for up to 8 hours before serving.

SERVES 8

WINE: A Prosecco from Bisol, Collalbrigo, or Fantinel or another sparkling wine would be delicious and refreshing here. A dry white such as Fiano di Avellino or Falanghina, both from Campania, or a Vermentino with bright acidity from Sardinia would work, too.

Rotolone d'uovo Meat-Filled Omelet Roll

6 eggs

1 tablespoon all-purpose flour

3 tablespoons grated Parmesan cheese

2 tablespoons whole milk

2 tablespoons minced fresh chives

2 teaspoons salt

2 tablespoons unsalted butter, or as needed

For the filling

¼ cup mayonnaise

1 rounded tablespoon Dijon mustard

2 tablespoons chopped cornichon (optional)

3 ounces thinly sliced cooked ham

3 ounces thinly sliced mortadella

A few handfuls of salad greens lightly dressed with a vinaigrette

You will need a good-sized sauté pan for making this antipasto, which results in a very pretty plate or platter when served. The pan size is important because the omelet must be large enough to stuff and roll. The roll can be prepared up to a day before serving, and then all you need to do is slice it. The slices are accompanied with a small green salad for a contemporary presentation.

o o o

In a bowl, whisk together the eggs, flour, cheese, milk, chives, and salt until well blended.

In a 12-inch sauté pan, melt the 2 tablespoons butter over medium heat. When the butter is hot, add the egg mixture and cook until golden on the underside, 3 to 4 minutes. Invert a platter or pizza pan slightly larger than the sauté pan over the pan and, holding the pan and platter together, flip them. Lift off the pan and return it to medium heat. If the pan looks dry, add a little more butter and allow it to melt. Slide the omelet back into the pan and cook just long enough to set the second side, 2 to 3 minutes. (If you do not feel you are agile enough to flip the omelet in this manner, you can slip the pan—make sure it is flameproof—under a preheated broiler for a few minutes, or into a preheated 350°F oven for 10 minutes, to set the top.) Slide the finished omelet onto a dish towel and let cool for about 10 minutes. The paler side (the side that was cooked first) should be facing up.

cont'd

To make the filling, in a small bowl, stir together the mayonnaise, mustard, and the cornichons, if using. Spread two-thirds of the mayonnaise mixture evenly over the top of the omelet. Top evenly first with the ham and then the mortadella. Spread the mortadella with the remaining mayonnaise mixture. Working carefully, roll up the omelet and place seam side down on a sheet of plastic wrap. Enclose the roll in the plastic wrap and then in aluminum foil. Refrigerate for at least 4 hours or for up to overnight.

To serve, cut the chilled omelet roll crosswise into 1/2-inch-thick slices. For individual service, place 2 slices on each plate and put a tiny mound of salad greens alongside. Or, arrange the omelet slices on a platter with a mound of salad in the center and let guests serve themselves. Serve at room temperature.

SERVES 8

WINE: With so many flavors in this dish (eggs, meat, mustard, cornichons), and perhaps on the antipasto table as well, it is wise to stay with wines that will work across a broad palette. Verdicchio from the Marche is a crowd-pleaser and pairs compatibly with many complex flavors. The minerally white wines from Campania, such as Falanghina, Greco di Tufo, and Fiano di Avellino, match nicely with many flavors and textures, too. For red wine, a non-*riserva* Rosso Conero from the Marche is a good choice. It has enough fruit balanced with great acidity to marry well with the eggs, meats, and cheese. Moroder makes a particularly good Rosso Conero.

Frittata di asparagi Asparagus Frittata

Extra-virgin olive oil as needed

Salt

1½ pounds thin asparagus spears, tough ends removed and cut into 1½-inch pieces

8 eggs

¼ cup whole milk, half-and-half, or heavy cream

1 tablespoon all-purpose flour (optional)

6 to 8 tablespoons grated Parmesan cheese

Pinch of freshly grated nutmeg or ground cinnamon

Freshly ground black pepper

¼ cup chopped green onions or green garlic (optional)

Slices of frittata are superb additions to nearly any antipasto table. Most recipes call for cooking the frittata on the stove top and flipping it to brown both sides, or browning the second side under the broiler. But baking the frittata is the easiest method and is practically foolproof. I have, however, included instructions for the combination of stove top and broiler for anyone who prefers to make it that way. Some cooks separate the eggs, beat the whites until they are stiff, and then fold them into the yolk-and-milk mixture for a slightly higher effect. I do not think the result is worth the extra step.

o o o

Preheat the oven to 350°F. Using about 1 tablespoon olive oil, liberally oil a 7-by-11-by-2-inch baking dish, or a 2-quart round baking dish if you prefer.

Bring a large pot of salted water to a boil, add the asparagus pieces, and cook until tender-crisp, 3 to 4 minutes. Drain well, refresh in cold water, and drain again.

In a bowl, whisk together the eggs, milk, flour (if using; it gives the frittata greater stability), cheese, nutmeg, 2 teaspoons salt, and several grinds of pepper.

If using the green onions, in a sauté pan, heat 2 tablespoons olive oil over low heat. Add the green onions and sauté for a few minutes to soften. Remove from the heat and stir into the egg mixture along with the asparagus. Pour the egg mixture into the prepared baking dish.

Bake the frittata until the top is set and lightly colored, 20 to 25 minutes. Remove from the oven, let cool for at least 8 to 10 minutes, and cut into squares or wedges. Serve warm or at room temperature.

Alternatively, after adding the green onions and asparagus to the egg mixture, heat 3 tablespoons olive oil in a 10-inch flameproof sauté pan over medium heat. When the oil is hot, add the egg mixture. Reduce the heat to low, cover, and cook until set, 10 to 15 minutes, or leave the heat at medium and cook uncovered for about 8 minutes. Meanwhile, preheat the broiler. When the frittata is set, slip it under the broiler for a few minutes to color the top lightly and to set any uncooked egg.

Remove from the broiler and run a knife around the sides of the pan to loosen the frittata. Invert a flat plate slightly larger than the sauté pan over the pan and, holding the pan and plate together, flip them. Lift off the pan and let the frittata cool for at least 10 minutes. Cut into wedges and serve warm or at room temperature.

SERVES 8 TO 12

Variations:

Artichokes: Use 4 large or 6 medium-sized cooked artichoke hearts, sliced lengthwise 1/4 inch thick, in place of the asparagus. Add 3 tablespoons chopped fresh mint or basil to the egg mixture.

Greens: Use 1 1/2 pounds assorted greens, such as escarole, Swiss chard, and spinach in any combination, trimmed, cooked, well drained, and chopped, in place of the asparagus. In place of the green onions, sauté 1/2 yellow onion, chopped, and 1 clove garlic, minced, in extra-virgin olive oil until softened and add to the egg mixture along with the greens.

Leeks: Use 4 to 6 large leeks, white and tender green, cut into 1-inch-thick slices, in place of the asparagus. Sauté in unsalted butter or extra-virgin olive oil until soft (about 2 cups).

Potatoes: Use 1 scant pound (4 small) potatoes, boiled, peeled, and sliced, in place of the asparagus. In place of the green onions, sauté 1 yellow onion, chopped, in extra-virgin olive oil until softened and add to the egg mixture along with the potatoes.

Mushrooms: Use 1 pound fresh mushrooms, stem ends trimmed, wiped clean, and sliced, in place of the asparagus. Sauté in extra-virgin olive oil with chopped fresh flat-leaf parsley, a little minced garlic, and a few drops of truffle oil, if desired, until tender.

Zucchini: Use 1 pound zucchini or 16 to 18 zucchini blossoms, or equal parts of each, in place of the asparagus. Trim and slice the zucchini and/or remove the stamens from the blossoms and halve or coarsely chop the blossoms. Blanch the zucchini slices and/or blossoms in boiling salted water for a minute or two, then drain well, refresh with cold water, and drain again.

WINE: Tocai Friulano, Sauvignon Blanc from Friuli or Alto Adige, or Ribolla from Friuli would complement the frittata, or pour a light red, like a Breganze Rosso or Merlot from the Veneto.

Caprino alla salsa rossa Goat Cheese with Spicy Tomato Sauce

For the sauce

2 teaspoons red pepper flakes

1/3 cup extra-virgin olive oil

2 cups peeled, seeded, and finely chopped plum tomatoes (fresh or canned)

1/2 cup tomato purée

1/4 cup red wine vinegar

Sugar, if needed

Salt and freshly ground black pepper

8 rounds fresh goat cheese, each 2 or 3 ounces

A few handfuls of salad greens dressed with extra-virgin olive oil (optional)

Toasted or grilled bread slices

Nothing could be simpler than coating a few rounds of cheese with a spicy tomato sauce. This Piedmontese classic, sometimes called *tomini elettrici,* or "electric cheese," will certainly stimulate your appetite. A *tomino* is a soft fresh cheese that is often made from cow's milk, but can be made from goat's milk or a combination of the two. Although this recipe calls for *caprino,* or a small fresh goat cheese, you may use any fresh cheese that you find at your market. Serve with slices of warm toast or grilled bread. Any extra sauce can be refrigerated and later served as an accompaniment to cooked beef or boiled or roasted chicken.

o o o

To make the sauce, in a small saucepan, heat the red pepper flakes in the olive oil over medium heat for a few minutes. Turn off the heat and let stand for a few minutes longer, so that the pepper flavor infuses the oil. Add the tomatoes, tomato purée, vinegar, and a little sugar for balance if the sauce seems too tart, place the pan over low heat, and bring the sauce to a simmer. Cook uncovered, stirring occasionally, until thickened, about 20 minutes.

Remove the sauce from the heat, season to taste with salt and pepper, and let cool completely. Taste again and adjust the seasoning.

Arrange the goat cheese rounds on salad plates and spoon the sauce evenly over the cheeses. For a contemporary touch, garnish the plates with some greens, if desired. Serve the bread on the side.

SERVES 8

WINE: Red wine is best here because of the forthright sauce. Try one from the Piedmont, such a juicy Dolcetto or a Nebbiolo d'Alba. A dry *spumante* would complement the sauce and cheese, too.

Sformato di gorgonzola e pere   Gorgonzola Custards with Pears

Unsalted butter for molds, plus
2 tablespoons

2 tablespoons all-purpose flour

1½ cups half-and-half, heated

2 whole eggs plus 2 egg yolks,
lightly beaten

½ pound Gorgonzola cheese,
crumbled, or to taste

Salt

For the vinaigrette

7 tablespoons walnut or hazelnut oil

2 tablespoons mild extra-virgin
olive oil

2 tablespoons balsamic vinegar

1 tablespoon sherry vinegar

Salt and freshly ground black
pepper

cont'd

This is a voluptuous starter course, but it would also be a great dessert for anyone who loves fruit and cheese to end a meal. The custards are creamy and mildly salty, a perfect match for a small salad of peppery greens accented with toasted nuts and slivers of ripe pear. Although this recipe will fill 6 standard custard cups, because the cheese custard is very rich, I suggest you fill 8 custard cups two-thirds full. Even though the presentation of these *sformati*, with their salad and fruit accompaniment, is contemporary, the Gorgonzola custards themselves are traditional preparations of Lombardy, where the cheese originates.

o o o

Preheat the oven to 350°F. Liberally butter eight ¾-cup custard cups or ramekins and place in a baking pan.

In a saucepan, melt the 2 tablespoons butter over medium heat. When the foam subsides, add the flour, stir well, and cook, stirring, for a minute or so to cook away the the raw taste of the flour. Slowly add the half-and-half while whisking constantly, and then cook, continuing

to whisk, until thickened enough to coat the back of a spoon, 3 to 5 minutes. Remove from the heat and gradually whisk in the whole eggs and egg yolks. Then whisk in the cheese until the mixture is smooth. Taste and add salt, if needed (the cheese will add salt). If you like, transfer the mixture to a small pitcher for easy pouring.

Pour the custard into the prepared custard cups. Carefully pour hot water into the baking pan to reach halfway up the sides of the molds. Cover the pan with aluminum foil. Bake the custards until a knife inserted into the center of a custard emerges clean, 25 to 30 minutes.

Meanwhile, make the vinaigrette: In a small bowl, whisk together all the oils and vinegars and then whisk in salt and pepper to taste. You will have about ¾ cup. Ready the remaining salad ingredients at the same time.

When the custards are ready, carefully remove the cups from the water bath and let rest for 5 minutes.

While the custards are resting, in a small bowl, toss the nuts with about 2 tablespoons of the vinaigrette. Set aside.

cont'd

1/2 cup walnuts or hazelnuts, toasted and coarsely chopped

2 bunches watercress, tough stems removed, or 3 cups arugula leaves

2 flavorful pears such as Anjou or Comice, unpeeled, halved, cored, and thinly sliced

Working with 1 custard at a time, run a knife blade around the inside of each mold to loosen the custard, then invert the custard onto a plate. When all the custards are unmolded, in a bowl, toss the watercress with all but about 1/4 cup of the remaining vinaigrette and divide among the plates. Top with the pear slices, again dividing evenly, and drizzle with the remaining vinaigrette. Sprinkle with the nuts. Serve immediately.

SERVES 8

NOTE: *You can bake these custards up to 1 day ahead of time, let cool, cover, and refrigerate. To warm them for serving, return the cups to the baking pan, add hot water to a depth of 1 inch to the pan, cover the baking pan, and heat in a preheated 350°F oven until the custards are warm in the center, 10 to 15 minutes. To test, insert a thin knife blade into a custard and withdraw it; the tip of the blade should feel warm to the touch. For a quicker method, reheat the custards in a microwave oven for 1 1/2 to 2 minutes.*

WINE: Moscato d'Asti is a refreshing choice, whether the custards are served as an antipasto or a dessert. Slightly effervescent and slightly sweet, it is the ideal match with the Gorgonzola and pears. Look for such producers as Saracco, Massolino, Braida, or Nivole.

Tartrà   Cheese and Onion Custard with Tomato Sauce

Unsalted butter for custard cups, plus 3 tablespoons

1/2 cup finely minced yellow onion

2 tablespoons all-purpose flour

2 cups half-and-half or equal parts whole milk and heavy cream, heated

4 eggs, lightly beaten

1 cup grated *groviera*, Gruyère, or Parmesan cheese, or a mixture

1 tablespoon chopped fresh black truffle or black truffle paste (optional; see note)

Salt and freshly ground black pepper

1 cup Tomato Sauce (page 42)

3 tablespoons heavy cream

Some food scholars believe the Piedmontese word *tartrà* is related to the Spanish *tarta*, a cake cooked in a round pan, but it is only conjecture. I have collected many different recipes for this classic Piedmontese flan, which is similar to what is called a *sformato* elsewhere in Italy. All have eggs but some have a great deal of cheese and others just a touch. Some are mostly onion-scented cream, and others play down the onion. My favorite *tartrà* recipe comes from chef Cesare Giaccone in Albaretto delle Torre, a village not far from Alba, in the heart of Piedmontese truffle country. He serves the truffle-accented custard with a light tomato sauce, but a sauce of sautéed mushrooms scented with truffle paste would be lovely, too. Or, you can skip the truffle in both the custard and the mushrooms, and still have a stunning antipasto. Also, I use a black truffle here, even though this is white truffle country. These custards, like the Gorgonzola custards in this chapter, can be made in advance and reheated; see the note on page 38 for directions.

○ ○ ○

Preheat the oven to 350°F. Liberally butter eight 3/4-cup custard cups and place in a baking pan.

In a small sauté pan, melt the 3 tablespoons butter over low heat. When the foam subsides, add the onion, and cook over low heat for 12 to 15 minutes. Add the flour, stir well, and cook, stirring, for a minute or so to cook away the raw taste of the flour. Slowly add the half-and-half while whisking constantly, and then cook, continuing to whisk, until thickened enough to coat the back of a spoon, 3 to 5 minutes. Remove from the heat and gradually whisk in the eggs. Then whisk in the cheese and the truffle paste, if using, until the mixture is smooth. Season to taste with salt and pepper. If you like, transfer the mixture to a small pitcher for easy pouring.

Pour the custard into the prepared custard cups. Carefully pour hot water into the baking pan to reach halfway up the sides of the molds. Cover the pan with aluminum foil. Bake the custards until a knife inserted into the center of a custard emerges clean, 25 to 30 minutes.

cont'd

When the custards are ready, carefully remove the cups from the water bath and let rest for 5 minutes. Meanwhile, heat the Tomato Sauce until hot and whisk in the cream. Working with one custard at a time, run a knife blade around the inside of each mold to loosen the custard, then turn the custard out onto a plate. Spoon the sauce around the custards and serve at once.

SERVES 8

NOTE: *Italian specialty stores carry different kinds of truffle paste. Some products are made from black truffles, some from white, and some mix truffles with porcini mushrooms. Some are a smooth purée and others are a bit chunky. The names vary as well: salsa al tartufo, crema di funghi al tartufo, truffle spread, and even truffle pâté. All of them will work in the recipes in this book.*

Variation: Osteria San Rocco in Izano, in Lombardy, serves a similar dish called *sformato di grana con fonduta di salva.* It omits the onion from the custard and serves the *sformato* with *fonduta* (page 105) made with *salva* cheese to which a few chopped sage leaves have been added.

WINE: Barbera or Dolcetto is the wine for this dish. If you choose Barbera, stay away from the more modern oaked versions, and instead pour a classic with medium-body, dark red fruit, and a backbone of acidity that delivers a freshness that will complement the custard. Look for such producers as Vietti, Massolino, or Renato Ratti. Or, look for a lively juicy, fruity Dolcetto from Villa Sparina, Poderi Colla, Anna Maria Abbona, or Ca'Viola.

salsa di pomodoro tomato sauce

1 can (28 ounces) plum tomatoes,
with juices

1/2 cup tomato purée

Salt and freshly ground black pepper

2 tablespoons unsalted butter, cut into
small pieces (optional)

You can use this sauce whenever you need a basic tomato sauce. It is easy to make and stores well in the refrigerator for up to 4 days. To transform it into a light tomato sauce, whisk in heavy cream, about 3 tablespoons for each cup of sauce, when reheating.

o o o

Pour the tomatoes and their juices into a food processor and process until finely chopped but not liquefied. Transfer to a heavy nonreactive saucepan, stir in the tomato purée, and place over low heat. Bring to a simmer and cook, stirring often, until the sauce is slightly thickened, 15 to 20 minutes.

Season to taste with salt and pepper and stir in the butter, if using. Use immediately, or let cool, cover, and refrigerate for up to 4 days.

MAKES 2 TO 2 1/2 CUPS

Fiori di zucchini fritti | Fried Zucchini Blossoms

For the filling

1/2 pound small zucchini

Salt

1/2 pound *scamorza* or fresh mozzarella cheese, finely diced

1 cup (about 1/2 pound) skim-milk or whole-milk ricotta cheese

6 tablespoons grated pecorino cheese

2 eggs, lightly beaten

1/4 cup chopped fresh basil, flat-leaf parsley, or marjoram, or a mixture

Freshly ground black pepper

18 to 24 zucchini blossoms

cont'd

You are lucky if you can go out into your garden and gather blossoms from your zucchini plants. I do not have that luxury where I live, but I do have an excellent farmers' market where I can buy young zucchini with their blossoms still attached, or I can purchase the larger male blossoms, which I prefer because they are easier to stuff.

If you buy your blossoms at a market, here is how to store these fragile beauties until you are ready to stuff them: lay them in a single layer on a baking sheet, cover them with a damp dish towel, and refrigerate for no longer than a day. Better yet, stuff them when you get them home. They will keep that way for up to a day in the refrigerator. The stuffed blossoms are rich, so allow two per person.

∘ ∘ ∘

To make the filling, grate the zucchini on the large holes of a box grater-shredder or with the large grater blade of a food processor. Place the zucchini in a colander, sprinkle with salt, and let stand for 30 minutes. Wrap the zucchini in a kitchen towel and squeeze dry.

In a bowl, combine the zucchini, cheeses, eggs, herb, and several grinds of pepper and mix well. (The filling can be assembled up to 1 day in advance of stuffing the blossoms, covered, and refrigerated.)

If the blossoms are wilted, soak in ice water for 15 minutes to recrisp them. Remove them from the water and lay them out on kitchen towels to absorb the water. Reach inside the center of each blossom, pinch off the stamen, and discard it.

Spoon the filling into a pastry bag fitted with a 1/2-inch plain tip, or into a heavy-duty plastic bag and cut off a bottom corner to create a 1/2-inch opening. (You can use a small spoon to fill the blossoms, but the process is very messy, making the pastry bag the easier choice.) Squeeze some of the filling into each blossom. Pinch the tops closed and set aside. (You can cover and refrigerate the stuffed blossoms for up to 1 day, but they are crispiest if stuffed and fried within a few hours.)

cont'd

For the batter

1 egg

1½ cups all-purpose flour

1 teaspoon salt

1½ to 2 cups ice water

Canola or other bland vegetable oil
or equal parts canola and olive oil
for deep-frying

Fleur de sel or coarse sea salt

To make the batter, whisk together the egg, flour, salt, and 1½ cups of the ice water. Add more ice water as needed to create a consistency that coats the back of a spoon. (You can make the batter up to 2 hours in advance, cover, and refrigerate it, but it will thicken as it rests. Add a little more water if necessary to correct the consistency.)

To fry the blossoms, preheat the oven to 200°F. Line an ovenproof tray with paper towels. Pour the oil to a depth of 3 inches into a heavy saucepan and heat to 350°F on a deep-frying thermometer. Holding a blossom by its stem, gently dip it into the batter, lift out, shake off the excess batter, and carefully lower the blossom into the hot oil. Repeat with more blossoms, adding only a few at a time to avoid crowding the pan. Fry the blossoms, turning gently if necessary to color evenly, until they are crisp and pale gold on all sides, about 4 minutes. Using a slotted spoon or wire skimmer, transfer the blossoms to the towel-lined tray to drain and keep warm in the oven. Repeat until all the blossoms are fried.

Arrange the blossoms on a platter and sprinkle with *fleur de sel*. Serve immediately.

MAKES 18 TO 24 STUFFED BLOSSOMS

Variation: To make a seafood filling for the blossoms, combine ½ pound fresh-cooked crabmeat or chopped cooked shrimp; ¼ cup finely chopped celery or fennel; ½ cup each skim-milk or whole-milk ricotta and finely shredded fresh mozzarella cheese; 1 egg, lightly beaten; 3 tablespoons each chopped fresh chives and flat-leaf parsley; finely grated zest of 1 large lemon; ½ teaspoon salt; several grinds of black pepper; and a pinch of cayenne pepper. Mix well, then pipe or spoon (this filling is not as messy to spoon) into the blossoms and fry as directed.

WINE: The wine needs to be both delicate and sturdy. Tocai Friulano from Scarbolo, Soave from Pieropan or Inama, and Verdicchio from Sartarelli are three good options. You can also pour a sparkling wine.

Torte Salate
Savory Pastries

Savory pastries are ideal antipasti for entertaining, as they can be prepared ahead of time and can be made as individual portions or served as slices cut from a larger pie, and most of them can be eaten hot, warm, or at room temperature. The pastry itself can be an olive oil–based dough, a buttery short crust, or a pizza or modified bread dough. Some Italian chefs, influenced by travel in France, have even started using puff pastry to enclose fillings.

Torte salate is one name for the traditional savory pies that, though served all over Italy, are a regional specialty of Liguria and Emilia-Romagna. In Liguria, the pastry is made with olive oil, delivering a rather elastic dough that develops a lovely crunch after emerging from the oven. In Emilia-Romagna, a region not known for culinary restraint, lard is added to the dough to make it richer. *Torte salate* are usually filled with vegetables and bound with cheese and eggs. A few conceal grains, making them more substantial and thus typically too heavy for antipasto.

Some *torte* have a single bottom crust with the sides of the pastry flipped over and partially covering the filling, much like a galette, while others have a top and a bottom crust. They also may be multilayered, in the manner of Greek filo pies. Although traditionally round, and baked in tart, pie, or springform pans for ease of serving, when volume is a consideration, *torte* may be baked in large rectangular pans and cut into squares.

Two other savory pastries are included in this chapter. Southern Italian *schiacciate,* which are double crusted and enclose a savory filling, resemble *torte* but are prepared with a pizza, rather than a pastry, dough. *Panzerotti,* which can be made with *torta* pastry, a buttery short crust, or pizza dough, are small filled pastries and usually deep-fried.

Finally, you will find a recipe for easy cheese biscotti, or crackers, fine partners for a glass of wine or a platter of prosciutto and melon. I have slipped some other simple bread-based antipasti, such as crostini, bruschette, and *tramezzini,* into Shop-and-Serve Antipasti.

Torta di zucca Butternut Squash Pie

For the filling

5 tablespoons unsalted butter

3 pounds butternut squash, peeled, seeded, and diced

1 yellow onion, chopped

2 cloves garlic, minced

2 tablespoons chopped fresh marjoram

1/2 ounce dried porcini mushrooms, soaked in hot water to cover for 30 minutes, drained, and chopped (optional)

3 eggs, lightly beaten

1 cup (about 1/2 pound) whole-milk ricotta or mascarpone cheese

2/3 cup grated Parmesan cheese

1 tablespoon salt

3/4 teaspoon freshly ground black pepper

3/4 teapoon freshly grated nutmeg

cont'd

I have served this pie at small, informal gatherings at home and to hundreds of guests at large fund-raising events. Why? *Complimenti!* Everyone loves this classic squash *torta* from Liguria. Its texture is robust but its flavor—butternut squash and nutmeg—is delicately sweet. The olive oil–based crust is easy to handle, plus it becomes nice and crisp after baking and never turns soggy as the pie cools.

Peeling a winter squash with its round contours and slick exterior, scooping out the seeds and fibers, and then trying to cut uniform dice can be challenging. My advice is to buy a butternut squash with the longest neck possible; it is easier to peel and has the greatest yield of solid flesh. Just cut the squash where the round seed-filled bottom part joins the neck, ideally with a heavy cleaver. Peel the neck, cut it crosswise with a cleaver or knife, and then dice the slices. You can discard the bottom because, after scraping out the seeds and trimming the thin, rounded walls, the yield is negligible. Squash contains a great deal of moisture, so after cooking, it is best to drain the squash purée for a few hours, even overnight if possible, before assembling the pie.

o o o

To make the filling, melt 4 tablespoons of the butter in a large saucepan over medium heat. Add the squash, onion, and water to a depth of 1/4 inch, cover, and cook until the squash and onion are very soft, about 25 minutes. (Check at the midpoint to see if the pan needs a bit more water; you do not want to scorch the squash.) Pass the contents of the pan through a food mill fitted with the coarse or medium blade or process in a food processor to a smooth purée. You should have about 3 cups purée. Put the purée in a sieve placed over a bowl and let drain for at least an hour or two or for up to overnight to rid it of excess moisture.

To make the pastry, in a bowl, stir together the flour and salt. Add the olive oil and most of the water and stir until the dough comes together in a rough mass, adding more water as needed. Alternatively, combine the flour and salt in a food processor, process briefly to mix, and then add the olive oil and water and pulse until a rough mass forms. Gather the dough into a ball and divide into 2 portions, one slightly larger than the other. Flatten each portion into a disk, cover with plastic wrap, and let rest for at least 30 minutes or up to 1 hour at room temperature. (The dough can be refrigerated for up to 1 day; bring it to room temperature before continuing.)

cont'd

For the pastry

3 cups unbleached all-purpose flour

1¹/₂ teaspoons salt

6 tablespoons olive oil

About ¹/₂ cup water or equal parts dry white wine and water

Olive oil for preparing pie pan

Fine dried bread crumbs for sprinkling

1 egg, lightly beaten, for brushing

To finish the filling, transfer the drained squash purée to a bowl. In a small sauté pan, melt the remaining 1 tablespoon butter over low heat. Add the garlic and marjoram and cook, stirring occasionally, for just a few minutes to soften the garlic's bite. Add to the squash along with the porcini (if using), eggs, and ricotta and Parmesan cheeses and mix well. Season with the salt, pepper, and nutmeg and mix again. (You can prepare the filling up to 1 day in advance, return it to the sieve placed over a bowl, and allow it to drain in the refrigerator until ready to use.)

Preheat the oven to 400°F. Oil a 9- or 10-inch pie pan.

On a lightly floured work surface, roll out the larger pastry disk into a 12-inch round about ¹/₄ inch thick. Carefully transfer the dough round to the oiled pie pan and ease it into the bottom and sides. Fold over the excess, creating about a ¹/₂-inch overhang and flatten it to make a rim. Roll out the second disk into a 10-inch round about ¹/₄ inch thick.

Sprinkle the bottom of the pastry-lined pan with a light, even coating of bread crumbs. Spoon the filling into the pan. Brush the edges of the bottom crust with the beaten egg, and carefully transfer the second dough round to the pan, laying it over the filling. Trim, if necessary, to make a neat edge, then turn the top and bottom edges under together and press to seal securely and make an attractive rim. Cut a few steam vents in the surface.

Brush the top crust with the beaten egg. Bake the pie for 30 to 40 minutes, or until the crust is golden. Remove from the oven and place on a wire rack to cool. Serve warm or at room temperature, cut into wedges.

SERVES 8 TO 12

WINE: A sparkling wine is once again a good match. Choose a great Prosecco di Valdobbiadene or a more substantial Franciacorta, which is made by the classic Champagne method. Some recommended Franciacorta producers are Bellavista, Contadi Castaldi, and Monte Rossa.

Erbazzone Spinach Pie from Emilia-Romagna

For the pastry

3 cups all-purpose flour

1 1/2 teaspoons salt

6 tablespoons olive oil, or 5 table-spoons lard and 3 tablespoons olive oil

1/2 cup water

For the filling

3 bunches (about 3 pounds) spinach, stems removed and coarsely chopped, to yield 12 cups, or a mixture of spinach and Swiss chard

2 tablespoons olive oil

1/2 pound pancetta, finely chopped

2 yellow onions, chopped

1 clove garlic, minced

1 teaspoon salt

1/2 teaspoon freshly ground black pepper

1/2 teaspoon freshly grated nutmeg, or to taste

cont'd

The famous—and beloved—greens-filled pie called *erbazzone* or *scarpazzone* is a signature dish of Emilia-Romagna. Pancetta is often added to the greens, and, having made this pie both with and without, I suggest you go with the pancetta. It adds a dimension of richness and contributes to a deeper flavor. While you can use a standard *torta* pastry, you may also want to try the richer dough of the region, which calls for a mixture of olive oil and lard.

Versions of this pie are also served in Lucca and Pisa, in Tuscany, and in Liguria, where *torta pasqualina* (Easter pie) is packed with spring greens. Milanese chef Gualtiero Marchesi uses puff pastry for his version, and cooks in Naples and in Sicily make a similar *torta,* but use escarole for the filling and season it more assertively with anchovies, capers, and olives. These pies are called *torta di scarola alla napoletana* and *impanata alla siciliana,* respectively, and both are delicious (see the variation that follows).

o o o

To make the pastry, in a bowl, stir together the flour and salt. Add the olive oil (or lard and oil) and most of the water and stir until the dough comes together in a rough mass, adding more water as needed. Alternatively,

combine the flour and salt in a food processor, process briefly to mix, and then add the olive oil (or lard and oil) and water and pulse until a rough mass forms. Gather the dough into a ball and divide into 2 portions, one slightly larger than the other. Flatten each portion into a disk, cover with plastic wrap, and let rest for at least 30 minutes or up to 1 hour at room temperature. (The dough can be refrigerated for up to 1 day; bring it to room temperature before continuing.)

To make the filling, in a large sauté pan, cook the spinach, with just the rinsing water clinging to the leaves, over medium heat until wilted and tender, 3 to 5 minutes. Transfer the spinach to a colander and press firmly against it with the back of spoon, forcing out as much moisture as possible. Chop finely, then squeeze the spinach dry in a dish towel to rid it of the last bit of moisture. You will have about 3 cups chopped greens. Set aside.

Rinse the sauté pan, dry, return to medium heat, and add the olive oil. Add the pancetta and cook, stirring occasionally, until the fat is rendered, about 3 minutes. Do not allow the pancetta to crisp. Add the onions and garlic and sauté until tender and pale gold, about 15 minutes. Add the cooked greens, mix well, and sauté for about 5 minutes to blend the flavors. Remove from the heat, season with the salt, pepper, and nutmeg, and let cool completely.

cont'd

3 eggs, lightly beaten

1/2 cup grated Parmesan cheese

Olive oil for preparing pie pan
and for brushing crust

Preheat the oven to 400°F. Oil a 9- or 10-inch pie pan.

On a lightly floured work surface, roll out the larger pastry disk into a 12-inch round about 1/4 inch thick. Carefully transfer the dough round to the oiled pie pan and ease it into the bottom and sides. Trim the overhang to about 1/2 inch. Roll out the second disk into a 10-inch round about 1/4 inch thick.

Spoon the greens mixture into the pastry-lined pan. Top evenly with the eggs and then with the cheese. Brush the edges of the bottom crust with olive oil, and carefully transfer the second dough round to the pan, laying it over the filling. Trim, if necessary, to make a neat edge, then turn the top and bottom edges under together and press to seal securely and make an attractive edge. Cut a few steam vents in the surface.

Brush the top crust with the olive oil. Bake the pie until the crust is golden, 30 to 35 minutes. Remove from the oven and place on a rack to cool. Serve warm or at room temperature, cut into wedges.

Variation: To make *torta di scarola alla napoletana,* prepare the pastry as directed, using olive oil. Trim and chop 3 heads escarole (about 3 pounds) and cook in lightly salted water until tender, 8 to 10 minutes. Drain well, refresh with cold water, and drain again, pressing out excess moisture. Chop finely, then squeeze the escarole dry in a dish towel to rid it of the last bit of moisture. You will have about 3 cups chopped greens. In a large sauté pan, heat 1/4 cup olive oil over low heat. Add 4 cloves garlic, minced; 8 olive oil–packed anchovy fillets, chopped; 3 tablespoons capers, rinsed and coarsely chopped; and 1/2 cup pitted black olives and sauté until the anchovies are melted, about 5 minutes. Add the escarole and cook, stirring, for 5 minutes to blend the flavors. Remove from the heat and add a pinch of red pepper flakes, if desired. Let cool for several minutes, then stir in 2 eggs, lightly beaten, to bind the filling. Let cool completely. Fill and bake the pie as directed for the spinach pie.

SERVES 8 TO 12

WINE: Tocai Friulano is the perfect white wine for many antipasti, including this spinach pie. You can also choose Lambrusco, a lightly sparkling—*frizzante*—wine with the flavor of dry cherries from the coast of Emilia-Romagna. Lambrusco is experiencing a small renaissance, and Ermete Medici is a particularly good producer.

The Neapolitan *torta* (see variation) calls for a wine that can stand up to the intensely flavored anchovies and capers. One suggestion is a Greco di Tufo from Campania. Another option is a white wine from Sicily that uses local grapes in the blend, rather than just Chardonnay. Look for the great white wine blends from Spadafora, Planeta, and Mirabile.

Torta di peperoni alla salsa di acciughe
Sweet Red Pepper Tart with Anchovy Cream

For the pastry

1 cup unbleached all-purpose flour

1/2 teaspoon salt

6 tablespoons chilled unsalted butter

2 tablespoons ice water, or as needed

For the filling

3 red bell peppers, roasted, peeled, seeded, and puréed (about 1 cup purée) (see note)

1 tablespoon tomato paste

3/4 cup whole milk or heavy cream

3 eggs, lightly beaten

1 tablespoon all-purpose flour

1/4 cup grated Parmesan cheese

Salt and freshly ground black pepper

cont'd

I first tasted a version of this tart at Garamond, a charming restaurant in Turin. It was presented as a tartlet, topped with two small, slightly spicy roasted green peppers and served with a creamy anchovy sauce. At home, I make a single large tart instead, which is less labor-intensive than rolling out individual tartlet crusts and is equally tasty. To match the slightly hot green pepper, I have suggested strips of roasted *poblanos.* If, however, your farmers' market has *pimientos de padrón,* small, mildly hot green chiles from Galicia, they would be ideal. They can be sautéed in olive oil at the last minute and sprinkled with *fleur de sel.*

o o o

To make the pastry, in a bowl, stir together the flour and salt. Add the butter and, using a pastry blender or 2 knives, cut it in until the mixture resembles coarse cornmeal. Add the 2 tablespoons ice water and gradually work it into the flour mixture with your fingers until the dough barely holds together, adding a little more ice water if needed. Do not overwork the dough, or it will be tough. Alternatively, combine the flour and salt in a food processor and process briefly to combine. Add the butter and pulse until the mixture resembles coarse cornmeal. With the motor running, add the 2 tablespoons ice water

and process just until the dough barely holds together, adding more ice water if needed. Gather the dough into a ball, pat it into a thick disk, wrap in plastic wrap, and refrigerate for at least 30 minutes or up to 1 day.

Preheat the oven to 425°F.

On a lightly floured work surface, roll out the dough into an 11-inch round about 1/8 inch thick. Carefully transfer the dough round to a 9-inch fluted tart pan with a removable bottom or a 9-inch pie pan and ease it into the bottom and sides. If using a tart pan, trim the overhang to make a neat edge, fold the overhang inward to reinforce the sides, and then run the rolling pin across the top of the pan to trim off the excess dough. If using a pie pan, trim the overhang to about 1/2 inch, fold the overhang under, and attractively flute the edge or leave it plain. (You can wrap the pastry-lined pan and keep it in the freezer for up to 1 day before baking.)

Line the pastry-lined pan with aluminum foil, allowing it to overhang the edge slightly, and fill with pie weights or dried beans. Bake for 15 minutes. Remove the weights and foil and bake until pale gold and the bottom is set, about 5 minutes longer. Remove from the oven and place on a wire rack to cool. Reduce the oven temperature to 375°F.

cont'd

For the anchovy cream

¼ cup olive oil

3 cloves garlic, chopped (optional)

8 olive oil–packed anchovy fillets, chopped

½ cup heavy cream, or as needed

Strips of roasted *poblano* or *padrón chiles* (optional)

To make the filling, in a bowl, whisk together the pepper purée, tomato paste, milk, eggs, flour, and cheese. Season generously with salt and pepper.

Pour the filling into the partially baked crust. Bake until the custard is set, about 25 minutes.

While the tart is baking, make the anchovy cream: In a small saucepan, combine the olive oil, garlic (if using), and anchovies and warm gently, stirring occasionally, until the anchovies melt into the oil. Whisk in the ½ cup cream and simmer gently until well blended. Taste and if the flavor is too strong, add a little more cream. Remove from the heat and reheat before serving.

Remove the tart from the oven and let cool on a wire rack for 10 minutes. Remove the sides of the tart pan and transfer the tart to a serving plate (or serve directly from the pan if you have used a pie pan). Cut into wedges and serve warm. Top each slice with a few strips of roasted chile, if using, and place a spoonful of anchovy cream on the side.

SERVES 8 TO 10

NOTE: *Although not authentic, jarred roasted Spanish* piquillo *peppers can be used in place of the bell peppers. They have a more intense perfume than the domestic bells.*

WINE: You cannot go wrong with a dry sparkling wine, either Prosecco or Franciacorta. You could also pair this antipasto with a ripe, flinty Gavi di Gavi. Look for Villa Sparina, one of the best producers.

Torte Salate 55 Savory Pastries

Schiacciata Double-Crusted Pizza

For the dough

2½ teaspoons (1 envelope) active dry yeast

½ cup warm water

3½ cups unbleached all-purpose flour

¾ cup cold water

3 tablespoons olive oil

1½ teaspoons salt

For the Calabrian filling

5 tablespoons olive oil

2 pounds tomatoes, peeled, seeded, and chopped, or 2 cans (14 ounces each) diced tomatoes, drained

3 tablespoons chopped garlic

3 tablespoons chopped fresh flat-leaf parsley

Long ago, Greeks ruled what are now Puglia, Calabria, and Sicily, and they left their culinary imprint on the local food. To this day, some of the double-crusted pies in these regions carry the Greek name *pitta,* rather than pizza. Others are called a *schiacciata,* meaning flattened or squashed. A yeast dough is used, and although it is remarkably easy to make, it needs time to rise. You can make the dough in advance and refrigerate it overnight. (Or, if really pressed for time, you can buy pizza dough in the refrigerated section at many markets.) You also have a choice of method, by hand or by stand mixer. (You can use a food processor, too, although the dough will require some meditative hand kneading once it is mixed). I like to make a dough that starts with a sponge, as it is relatively foolproof and gives the yeast a head start.

∘ ∘ ∘

To make the dough, in a large bowl or the large bowl of a stand mixer, dissolve the yeast in the warm water and let stand until foamy, about 5 minutes. Add ½ cup of the flour and stir to combine. This is the sponge. Cover the bowl with a kitchen towel and let the sponge rest at room temperature until bubbly, about 30 minutes.

Add the remaining 3 cups flour, the cold water, the olive oil, and the salt to the sponge. If making by hand, stir with a wooden spoon until the ingredients come together to form a dough, and then turn out onto a lightly floured work surface and knead until soft and smooth, about 10 minutes. If using a stand mixer, fit it with the dough hook and mix the ingredients on low speed until the dough leaves the sides of the bowl cleanly, about 10 minutes.

Gather the dough into a ball, transfer it to an oiled bowl, turn the ball to coat the surface with oil, cover the bowl with plastic wrap, and let the dough rise in a warm place until doubled in bulk, about 1 hour.

Turn the dough out onto a lightly flour work surface, punch down, divide in half, and shape into 2 balls. Place the balls on a floured baking sheet, cover with a kitchen towel or plastic wrap, and refrigerate for at least 30 minutes or up to overnight.

Bring the dough to room temperature. Position an oven rack in the lowest rung in the oven and preheat to 500°F. If you have tiles or a pizza stone, place it on the rack at the same time and preheat for at least 30 minutes. If you do not, have ready a large rimmed baking sheet or a pizza pan 14 inches in diameter.

6 olive oil–packed anchovy fillets, chopped (about 2 tablespoons)

½ cup pitted oil-cured black olives, chopped

1 tablespoon capers, rinsed and drained

1 can (6 ounces) olive oil–packed tuna, drained

For the Pugliese filling

2 cups (about 15 ounces) fresh whole-milk ricotta cheese, spooned into a sieve and allowed to drain in the refrigerator for 1 hour

½ teaspoon salt

¼ pound salami, chopped

2 ounces *ricotta salata* or provolone cheese, grated

3 hard-boiled eggs, peeled and chopped

Olive oil for brushing

Select one of the fillings. To make the Calabrian filling, in a large sauté pan, heat 3 tablespoons of the olive oil over medium heat. Add the tomatoes and garlic and cook, stirring, until slightly thickened, about 5 minutes. Remove from the heat and let cool slightly before using. In a small sauté pan, heat the remaining 2 tablespoons olive oil over medium heat. Add the anchovies and when they just begin to melt, add the parsley, olives, capers, and tuna and mix well. Remove from the heat.

If making the Pugliese filling, have all the ingredients ready.

On a lightly floured work surface, using your hands, stretch half of the dough into a round about 14 inches in diameter. Repeat with the second dough ball to form a second round the same size.

Transfer 1 dough round to a baker's peel if using tiles or a stone, or to the baking sheet or pizza pan if not. If using the Calabrian filling, spread the tomato mixture over the round, leaving the edges uncovered. Spoon the tuna mixture evenly over the top. Top with the second dough round and pinch the edges together to seal.

If using the Pugliese filling, combine the fresh ricotta with the salt and spread the fresh ricotta evenly over the round, leaving the edges uncovered. Top evenly with the salami, the *ricotta salata,* and finally the eggs. Top with the second dough round and pinch the edges together to seal.

Brush the top of the *schiacciata* with olive oil, then, if using the baker's peel, slide the *schiacciata* onto the stone. Or, place the baking sheet or pizza pan with the *schiacciata* into the hot oven. Bake until golden brown, 18 to 20 minutes.

If using a pizza stone, remove the *schiacciata* from the oven with the baker's peel and slide it onto a wire rack. If using a baking sheet or pizza pan, transfer the pan to the rack. Let cool for at least 15 minutes. Serve warm or at room temperature, cut into wedges.

SERVES 8 TO 10

NOTE: *You can use the same dough for making pizza; this amount will yield one 13-by-15-inch rectangular crust, two 12- or 13-inch round crusts, or four 7-inch round crusts.*

WINE: For the Calabrian filling with tuna, pour Falanghina, the ripe, minerally, melon-flavored white from Campania. For the Pugliese filling with ricotta, drink a Primitivo, a hearty, smoky, jammy red wine that will complement the intense flavor of the salami. Look for Primitivo producers such as Feudi Monaci, Luccarelli, and Accademia dei Racemi.

Panzerotti Fried Stuffed Pastries

For the pastry

2 3/4 cups unbleached all-purpose flour

1 teaspoon salt

4 tablespoons chilled unsalted butter

2 egg yolks, lightly beaten

2/3 to 3/4 cup ice water

For the Neapolitan cheese and ham filling

2/3 cup finely shredded *groviera* or Gruyère cheese

1/2 cup grated Parmesan cheese

3 ounces chopped cooked ham, prosciutto, or salami (optional)

1 egg, lightly beaten

2 tablespoons chopped fresh flat-leaf parsley

2 tablespoons chopped fresh basil or marjoram

cont'd

Panzerotti (sometimes spelled *panzarotti*) are classic small fried pastries popular in southern Italy. When a pastry is fried, it swells up and looks like a *pancia,* or full tummy, hence, the name. These savory finger foods can be assembled ahead of time and refrigerated for up to 1 day or frozen for up to 1 month. (If you freeze them, thaw at room temperature before frying.) I have included a butter-based short crust pastry here, but you can also use the *torta* pastry dough on page 48 or the *schiacciata* dough on page 56. Select one of the fillings to make. If you have fear of frying, you can brush the pastries with egg wash and bake them in a preheated 375°F oven until golden, about 20 minutes.

o o o

To make the pastry, in a bowl, stir together the flour and salt. Add the butter and, using a pastry blender or 2 knives, cut it in until the mixture resembles coarse cornmeal. Add the egg yolks and 2/3 cup ice water and stir and toss with a fork until the dough barely holds together, adding a little more ice water if needed. Alternatively, combine the flour and salt in a food processor and process briefly to combine. Add the butter and pulse

until the mixture resembles coarse cornmeal. With the motor running, add the egg yolks and 2/3 cup ice water and process just until the dough barely holds together, adding more ice water if needed. Gather the dough into a ball, pat it into a thick disk, wrap in plastic wrap, and refrigerate for at least 30 minutes or up to 1 day.

Select one of the fillings. In a bowl, combine the ingredients for the chosen filling and mix well. Or, combine the ingredients in the food processor and pulse briefly to mix.

On a lightly floured work surface, roll out the dough 1/4 inch thick, or thinner if possible. Using a 3-inch round cookie cutter or similar tool, cut out as many rounds as possible. Gather together the dough scraps, reroll them, and cut out as many additional rounds as possible. You should have 30 to 36 rounds.

Line 2 rimmed baking sheets with parchment paper. Place a heaping teaspoonful of the filling in the center of each dough round. Brush the edges of the dough round with egg white, fold in half, and pinch to seal. As each pastry is formed, place on a prepared baking sheet and leave until ready to fry.

cont'd

For the Pugliese cheese and salami filling

1/4 pound fresh mozzarella cheese, finely diced

1/2 cup grated Parmesan cheese

3 ounces salami, finely diced

2 eggs, lightly beaten

For the Neapolitan all-cheese filling

1/4 pound fresh mozzarella cheese, finely diced

2 ounces smoked provolone cheese, finely diced

1/2 cup grated Parmesan cheese

1 egg, lightly beaten

1/4 cup chopped fresh flat-leaf parsley

1 egg white, lightly beaten, for brushing

Canola or other bland vegetable oil or equal parts canola and olive oil for deep-frying

Preheat the oven to 200°F. Line an ovenproof tray with paper towels. Pour oil to a depth of 2 inches into a deep sauté pan or saucepan and heat to 350°F on a deep-frying thermometer. When the oil is hot, add the filled pastries, a few at a time, and fry until golden, about 4 minutes. Using a slotted spoon or wire skimmer, transfer the pastries to the towel-lined tray to drain and keep warm in the oven. Repeat until all the pastries are fried.

Arrange the pastries on a platter and serve hot.

MAKES 30 TO 36 PASTRIES

WINE: You need a wine to play off the richness of these savory pastries. Verdicchio, the flinty, crisp white from the Marche, will work well, as will Greco di Tufo from Campania. For something very crisp and light, you can open an Orvieto. And a sparkling wine would be good, too.

Biscotti di parmigiano Parmesan Crackers

1½ cups unbleached all-purpose flour

1 cup grated Parmesan cheese

½ cup (¼ pound) chilled unsalted butter, cut into 1-tablespoon slices, plus butter for preparing baking sheets (optional)

2 teaspoons freshly ground coarse black pepper

1 egg, lightly beaten

While doing research for my book *Sephardic Flavors,* I came across a recipe for biscuits (*boyikos de keso*) prepared with kasseri cheese and red pepper flakes. Since then, I have made them often to serve to guests before a meal, and they have always been a big hit. One day, while reading the *New York Times* food section, I saw a recipe for a cheese cracker from a Signora Mustilli from Campania. Of course, I had to try it. Her crackers resembled the Sephardic recipe, but were a bit darker because they were double baked, like many sweet biscotti. I entered a phase of biscotti madness, trying many variations. In this recipe, I have added black pepper to a basic Parmesan dough, as I loved the subtle buzz of heat in the Sephardic cheese cracker. (You may cut back on the pepper, but I think you will like it as is.) I have included two variations as well—both delicious, so I could not leave them out. These are perfect crackers to serve with a bowl of olives or a plate of prosciutto and a glass of sparkling wine.

○ ○ ○

In a food processor, combine the flour and Parmesan and process briefly to combine. Add the butter and pepper and pulse until the mixture is crumbly. Add the egg and pulse again until the mixture comes together.

Turn the dough out onto a sheet of plastic wrap. Shape into a log about 2 inches in diameter, and then enclose the log in the plastic wrap. Refrigerate the log until firm, at least 3 hours or up to overnight.

Preheat the oven to 375°F. Butter 2 rimmed baking sheets, or line the baking sheets with parchment paper.

Unwrap the dough log and cut crosswise into ¼-inch-thick slices. Arrange the slices on the baking sheets about 1 inch apart. Bake the crackers until firm but still very pale, 15 to 18 minutes. Remove from the oven. They are lovely as they are, and you can simply transfer the crackers to wire racks to cool. But if you want to try the second-bake technique, raise the oven temperature to 500°F. When the oven is ready, return the baking sheets to the oven and bake the crackers until golden brown, about 3 minutes longer.

Transfer the crackers to a wire rack and let cool completely. Store in an airtight container for up to 1 week. If desired, warm slightly in a 300°F oven before serving.

MAKES ABOUT 24 CRACKERS

cont'd

Variations:

Biscotti di formaggio e mandorle **(Almond Cheese Crackers):** In a food processor, combine 1 1/2 cups unbleached all-purpose flour, 1 cup grated Parmesan cheese, 1/2 teaspoon salt, and 1/4 teaspoon freshly grated nutmeg and process briefly to mix. Add 1/2 cup (1/4 pound) chilled unsalted butter, cut into 1-tablespoon slices, and pulse until the mixture resembles coarse meal. Add 1 egg, lightly beaten, and pulse just until the dough starts to come together. Add 1/2 cup slivered blanched almonds and pulse briefly just to combine. Pat into a log 2 inches in diameter, wrap in plastic wrap, and refrigerate until firm, at least 3 hours. Slice and bake as directed but omit the second bake. Makes about 30 crackers.

Biscotti di gorgonzola e noce **(Gorgonzola and Walnut Crackers):** In a food processor, combine 1/2 cup (1/4 pound) unsalted butter and 6 ounces Gorgonzola cheese, both at room temperature. Pulse to soften and combine. Add 2 cups all-purpose unbleached flour, 1/4 teaspoon freshly grated nutmeg, 1 1/2 teaspoons salt, and 1 or 2 grinds of black pepper and process to combine. Add 1 egg, lightly beaten, and pulse just until the dough starts to come together. Add 1/2 cup walnuts and

pulse briefly to combine. Pat into a log 2 inches in diameter, wrap in plastic wrap, and refrigerate until firm, at least 3 hours. Slice and bake as directed but omit the second bake. Makes about 36 crackers.

WINE: Open a bottle of Prosecco from Collalbrigo, Bisol, Ruggeri, or Dea. Or, consider a Tocai Friulano—particularly good if you are serving prosciutto as well—or a Soave Classico. If Tocai is your choice, look for Scarbolo, Bastianich, Movia, Antico Broilo, or Venica & Venica. Inama, Corte Sant'Alda, Gini, Pieropan, and Pra are excellent Soave producers.

Farinaci
Grains

The most common grains used for making antipasti are rice, cornmeal, and *farro,* but because they can be filling, the dishes are always served in small portions. Rice typically turns up in the form of croquettes. Italians grow short-grain rice, with Carnaroli (the largest grain), Arborio (a medium grain), and Vialone Nano (the smallest grain) the three best-known varieties and all used for making risotto. For croquettes, I recommend Arborio. It is the most widely sold of the three and its medium-sized grains absorb a great deal of liquid while remaining al dente at the center. For salads, I like to use Carnaroli because the kernels are a bit larger, although Arborio works well, too.

Most Italian cornmeal, or polenta, is golden yellow, stone ground, and available in fine, medium, and coarse grinds. The Venetians prefer white polenta, which has less corn flavor. For most recipes, such as the Fried Polenta with Cheese Spread on page 72, I like to use medium-grind yellow polenta because it has a full flavor and a subtle crunch, but I have included a polenta cake from Abruzzo (page 75) that is generally made with coarse-grind polenta.

Finally, *farro,* an early variety of wheat sometimes erroneously labeled spelt, is primarily cultivated around Lucca in the Garfagnana area of Tuscany, in Umbria, and in Abruzzo. In the past, it needed to be picked over for stones and grit, soaked overnight, and cooked for a long time, but nowadays this ancient grain is well cleaned and partially abraded, so that it usually cooks in less than a half hour. Its nutty taste and texture recalls barley more than wheat, and it makes an excellent antipasto salad.

Crocchetti di riso Rice Croquettes

For the rice mixture

3 1/2 cups water

1/2 teaspoon chopped saffron threads, steeped in 1/4 cup hot water for 15 minutes (optional)

1 1/2 teaspoons salt

2 cups Arborio rice

2 eggs

2/3 cup grated Parmesan cheese

1/4 teaspoon freshly ground black pepper

For the *arancine* filling

3 tablespoons olive oil

5 to 6 ounces beef or part beef and part pork, not too lean, finely chopped or ground

1/2 yellow onion, chopped

cont'd

Italians are addicted to all manner of rice croquettes. Some *crocchetti* are the product of leftover risotto; others are prepared on purpose, just for their own crunchy goodness. There are small, flattened cakes; little round balls, which may or may not be stuffed with cheese; *arancine,* usually round jumbo-sized croquettes; and *suppli,* oval croquettes. The rice may be tinted with saffron or not.

The simplest round croquette may enclose a cube of mozzarella or Fontina, possibly dipped in chopped herbs. In Rome, *suppli al telefono* are the croquettes of choice. No saffron is used in the rice, and the stuffing is a mixture of chopped prosciutto, porcini mushrooms, a bit of tomato paste, and mozzarella. When a hot *suppli* is bitten into and then drawn away from the mouth, the melted cheese forms long, stringlike strands that recall old-fashioned telephone cords from the days before the era of the *telefonino* (cell phone). In Sicily, where *arancine* are a specialty, cooks often stuff them with peas and finely chopped meat.

While croquettes can be mixed and shaped well ahead of time and refrigerated, cooking them is a last-minute event. Be sure any other antipasti you have on the menu can be fully prepared ahead, leaving you free to fry the croquettes.

∘∘∘

To make the rice mixture, in a saucepan, combine the water, saffron infusion (if using), and 1 teaspoon of the salt and bring to a boil over high heat. Add the rice, stir well, reduce the heat to low, and cover the pan. Cook until the rice has absorbed all of the water and is cooked through but still sticky, about 15 minutes. Remove from the heat and let cool for a few minutes. Stir in the eggs and cheese and season with the remaining 1/2 teaspoon salt and the pepper. Spoon the rice out onto a rimmed baking sheet, spreading it evenly so that it cools quickly. Refrigerate until cold but not hard, 1 to 2 hours.

While the rice chills, choose one of the fillings. To make the *arancine* filling, in a sauté pan, heat the olive oil over medium heat. Add the meat, onion, carrot, and celery and sauté until golden, about 15 minutes. Add the tomato sauce and diluted tomato paste, reduce the heat to low, and cook, stirring occasionally, until thick, about 30 minutes. Remove from the heat and fold in the peas, if using. Transfer to a bowl, let cool completely, cover, and chill well.

cont'd

1 small carrot, peeled and chopped

1 small celery stalk, chopped

1 cup tomato sauce, homemade
(page 42, made without cream)
or purchased

1 tablespoon tomato paste, diluted
in 1 tablespoon warm water

1/4 cup English peas, cooked (optional)

For the *supplì al telefono* filling

2 tablespoons olive oil

1/2 cup chopped yellow onion

1 teaspoon finely minced garlic

5 to 6 ounces ground beef (optional)

2 tablespoons dried porcini mushrooms, soaked in 1/3 cup hot water
for 30 minutes, drained, with liquid
reserved, and finely chopped (to
yield about 1/4 cup chopped porcini)

1/4 cup diced prosciutto

2 teaspoons tomato paste, diluted
in 1 tablespoon warm water

To make the the *supplì al telefono* filling, in a sauté
pan, heat the olive oil over medium heat. Add the onion
and sauté until soft and translucent, about 10 minutes.
Add the garlic and the ground beef, if using, and sauté
until the beef is no longer red, about 5 minutes. Add
the mushrooms and their soaking liquid, the prosciutto,
and the tomato paste and simmer until the mixture is
thick, about 15 minutes. Season to taste with salt and
pepper. Transfer to a bowl and let cool completely. Have
the mozzarella cheese ready.

To shape and stuff the croquettes, line 2 rimmed baking
sheets with parchment paper. Dampen your hands with
water. Scoop up a spoonful of the rice and shape into a
2 1/2-inch ball if making *arancine* or an oval 2 1/2 inches
long and about 1 1/2 inches in diameter if making *supplì*.
With an index finger, make an indentation in the rice
and spoon some of the filling into the center. If making
the *supplì*, tuck in a cube of mozzarella, too. Smooth the
rice over the filling, reshaping the croquette, and place
on a parchment-lined baking sheet. Repeat until all the
rice is used, continuing to dampen your hands as you
work so the rice does not stick to your fingers.

Pour the flour and bread crumbs each into its own
shallow bowl. Break the eggs into a third shallow bowl
and beat lightly until blended. One at a time, dip the
croquettes in the flour, then in the eggs, and finally in
the bread crumbs, coating evenly each time, and place
on the second parchment-lined baking sheet. Cover and
refrigerate until fully chilled, at least 2 hours or up to
24 hours.The croquettes are easier to fry if they are fully
chilled, which firms them up.

Preheat the oven to 200°F. Line an ovenproof tray with
paper towels. Pour oil to a depth of 3 inches into a
heavy saucepan and heat to 350°F on a deep-frying thermometer. Place a few croquettes on a wire skimmer,
slip them into the hot oil, and fry until golden brown,
lifting them out of the oil a few times so that the filling
can become hot. This step is especially important for the
supplì. As you fry, lift the balls out of the hot oil with
the wire skimmer, hold them for a minute, and then slip
them back into the hot oil. Repeat this process twice. If
you do not do this, the *supplì* will be golden on the outside but the mozzarella will remain solid. It should take
6 to 7 minutes total to fry the croquettes. Using the wire
skimmer, transfer the croquettes to the towel-lined tray
to drain and keep warm in the oven for up to 15 minutes.
Repeat until all the croquettes are cooked.

Salt and freshly ground black pepper

1/2 pound fresh mozzarella cheese, cut into 3/4-inch cubes

1 cup all-purpose flour

1 cup fine dried bread crumbs

2 eggs

Olive oil or equal parts olive and canola oil for deep-frying

Arrange the croquettes on a platter and serve piping hot. Do not forget the napkins. This is finger food.

MAKES 12 TO 16 CROQUETTES

Variation:
You can also stuff the croquettes with cheese only. Cut 1/2 pound fresh mozzarella or Fontina cheese into 1/2-inch cubes, form the rice mixture into balls 11/2 inches in diameter, and stuff 1 cube of cheese into each ball. Coat and fry as directed, reducing the frying time by a minute or two because of the smaller size.

WINE: My first choice would be to reach for a glass of bubbly, whether it is Prosecco, Franciacorta, or an interesting *spumante* from your favorite region. You cannot go wrong unless your selection is too sweet. Look for producers such as Collalbrigo, Sorelle Bronca, or Ruggeri. Other possibilities include aromatic, minerally whites. Falanghina from such Campanian wineries as Vesevo and Terredora is a satisfying choice.

Crocchetti di riso al tartufo nero
Truffled Rice Croquettes from Umbria

For the rice mixture

2 tablespoons unsalted butter or extra-virgin olive oil

1/2 yellow onion, finely chopped

1 carrot, peeled and finely chopped

1 celery stalk, finely chopped

1 sweet Italian sausage, about 3 ounces, casing removed and crumbled

1 cup Arborio rice

2 cups chicken stock

1 egg, lightly beaten

Grated zest of 1 lemon

1/4 cup grated Parmesan cheese

1 black truffle, grated or finely chopped, or 1 tablespoon black truffle paste (see note, page 41)

Umbria is known for its black truffles. Here, the rice for the croquettes is started as if you are making a risotto, but the liquid is added all at once. Aromatic vegetables, sausage, and truffle are added to the rice, and stock is used instead of water for a deeper flavor. There is no filling, just the perfume of truffles.

o o o

To make the rice mixture, in a sauté pan, melt the butter over medium heat. Add the onion, carrot, and celery and sauté until soft, about 10 minutes. Add the sausage meat and stir until the meat loses it raw pinkness and becomes very lightly browned. Add the rice and stir until opaque, 2 to 3 minutes. Add the stock all at once and cook, uncovered, until the stock is just absorbed by the rice, about 10 minutes. Remove from the heat and let cool for 5 to 10 minutes.

Add the egg, lemon zest, cheese, and truffle to the rice and mix well. Spoon the rice out onto a rimmed baking sheet, spreading it evenly so that it cools quickly. Refrigerate until cold but not hard, 1 to 2 hours.

To shape the croquettes, line 2 rimmed baking sheets with parchment paper. Dampen your hands with water. Scoop up a spoonful of the rice, shape into a 1 1/2-inch ball between your palms, and place on a parchment-lined baking sheet. Repeat until all the rice is used, continuing to dampen your hands as you work so the rice does not stick to your fingers.

Pour the flour and bread crumbs each into its own shallow bowl. Break the eggs into a third shallow bowl and beat lightly until blended. One at a time, dip the croquettes in the flour, then in the eggs, and finally in the bread crumbs, coating evenly each time, and place on the second parchment-lined baking sheet. Cover and refrigerate until fully chilled, at least 2 hours or up to 24 hours. The croquettes are easier to fry if they are fully chilled, which firms them up.

1 cup all-purpose flour

1 cup fine dried bread crumbs

2 eggs

Olive oil or equal parts olive and
canola oil for deep-frying

Preheat the oven to 200°F. Line an ovenproof tray with paper towels. Pour oil to a depth of 3 inches into a heavy saucepan and heat to 350°F on a deep-frying thermometer. Place a few croquettes on a wire skimmer, slip them into the hot oil, and fry until golden brown, about 4 minutes. Using the wire skimmer, transfer the croquettes to the towel-lined tray to drain and keep warm in the oven for up to 15 minutes. Repeat until all the croquettes are cooked.

Arrange the croquettes on a platter and serve piping hot. Do not forget the napkins. This is finger food.

MAKES ABOUT 32 CROQUETTES

WINE: Here is another opportunity to pour a good sparkling wine. If you prefer a still white, try a glass of Orvieto, a local favorite in Umbria. Some red options are Morellino di Scansano from Tuscany's southwest coast—look for the producer Fattoria Le Pupille—or choose a Montefalco Rosso, a Sangiovese blend from Umbria, from Arnaldo Caprai or Adanti.

Polenta fritta con crema di formaggio
Fried Polenta with Cheese Spread

Extra-virgin olive oil for preparing pan, plus oil for frying

1 cup medium-grind polenta (about 5½ ounces)

4 cups water

Salt and freshly ground black pepper

4 tablespoons unsalted butter (optional)

½ pound fresh *robiola cheese,* at room temperature

5 ounces *gorgonzola dolcelatte* cheese, at room temperature

¼ pound mascarpone cheese

Whole milk as needed

¼ cup chopped toasted walnuts (optional)

All-purpose flour and/or fine dried bread crumbs for dusting (optional)

1 egg (optional)

Gabriele Trisoglio, at her restaurant La Pomera in Vignale Monferrato, in the Piedmont, serves an antipasto of fried polenta with a rich cheese spread and often pairs it with a salad of Belgian endive, celery, or fennel. Chopped walnuts are sometimes added to the cheese mixture. Or, you could add walnuts to the salad and dress it with a walnut vinaigrette (page 36).

○○○

Oil a 9-by-12-inch rimmed baking sheet.

In a heavy saucepan, whisk together the polenta and water and place over medium heat. Bring slowly to a boil, whisking often to prevent lumps from forming. Reduce the heat to low and simmer uncovered, stirring often, until the polenta is thick and no longer grainy on the tongue, 20 to 30 minutes. Whisk in salt and pepper to taste and the butter, if using. Turn the polenta out onto the prepared baking sheet and spread into an even layer. It should be about 1/4 inch thick. Let cool, cover, and refrigerate until firm.

In a food processor, combine the cheeses and process until smooth. Add milk as needed to make a spreadable mixture and fold in the walnuts, if using. Season to taste with salt and pepper. Transfer to a bowl, cover, and refrigerate until needed.

Remove the polenta from the refrigerator and invert onto a cutting board. Cut into desired shapes—small squares, triangles, rounds, or rectangles. You can fry the polenta cutouts as they are, or you can dust them lightly and evenly with flour. Or, pour some flour and bread crumbs each into its own shallow bowl. Break the egg into a third shallow bowl and beat lightly until blended. One at a time, dip the polenta pieces in the flour, then in the egg, and finally in the bread crumbs, coating evenly each time, and place on a baking sheet lined with parchment paper.

Preheat the oven to 200°F. Line an ovenproof tray with paper towels. Pour olive oil to a depth of about ¹/₂ inch into a large sauté pan and heat to 350°F on a deep-frying thermometer. Add the polenta pieces, in batches, and fry, turning once, until golden on both sides, 4 to 5 minutes total. Using a slotted spoon, transfer the fried polenta to the towel-lined tray to drain and keep warm in the oven. Repeat until all the polenta is fried.

Place the cheese mixture in the center of a round platter and surround with the pieces of polenta. Serve while the polenta is hot.

SERVES 4

Variation:

You can make the polenta as directed and cut into small squares. Spread half of the squares with the cheese mixture and top with the remaining squares. Pour olive oil or equal parts olive and canola oil to a depth of 3 inches into a heavy saucepan and heat to 350°F on a deep-frying thermometer. Working with a few polenta sandwiches at a time, dip them first into beaten egg and then into flour (or some cooks reverse the order) and slip them into the hot oil. Fry, turning once, until golden, about 4 minutes total. Remove with a slotted spoon or wire skimmer to paper towels to drain, and repeat until all the sandwiches are fried. Serve warm.

WINE: Choose Dolcetto or Barbera, two delicious grapes from Piedmont that come in many styles. Look for a young, approachable wine, rather than a big, oak-influenced one. Producers to seek out are Massolino, Vietti, Villa Sparina, Anna Maria Abbona, Oberto, and Ceretto.

Pizza di granturco Crisp Polenta Cake

Olive oil for preparing skillet

2 cups coarse- or medium-grind polenta (about 11 ounces)

6 cups water

Salt and freshly ground black pepper

For the spicy greens

Salt

2 pounds assorted bitter greens such as escarole, kale, dandelion, Swiss chard, or broccoli rabe, tough stems removed

1/4 cup extra-virgin olive oil

3 to 5 cloves garlic, chopped

1 to 2 tablespoons red wine vinegar

Red pepper flakes

Grated pecorino or shredded smoked provolone or *scamorza* cheese for topping

Pizza di granturco, a specialty of the Abruzzo, is all about texture. The polenta cake is crisp and crunchy from the coarse grind of the cornmeal and from the baking technique. (If you can find only medium-grind polenta, you can use it, but the cake will not be as crunchy.) I usually serve the cake topped with cooked greens, but it can be a vehicle for many different toppings, such as those you might serve on crostini (see variations).

∘ ∘ ∘

Preheat the oven to 400°F. Liberally oil a well-seasoned 12-inch cast-iron skillet or a 12-inch round baking dish and place in the oven for a few minutes to heat. Heating the pan or dish is important, as it helps the polenta form a bottom crust.

In a heavy saucepan, whisk together the polenta and water and place over medium heat. Bring slowly to a boil, whisking often to prevent lumps from forming. Reduce the heat to low and simmer uncovered, stirring occasionally, for just a few minutes until smooth. Season with salt and black pepper and carefully pour into the hot prepared skillet or dish.

Bake the polenta cake until it pulls away from the sides of the pan and is lightly golden, 30 to 40 minutes. The cake will be crisp.

While the polenta cake is baking, prepare the spicy greens: Bring a large pot of salted water to a boil, add the greens, and boil until very tender, 15 to 20 minutes. Drain the greens into a colander, pressing firmly on them with the back of a spoon to force out excess moisture. Chop the greens coarsely. In a sauté pan, heat the olive oil over medium heat. Add the garlic and the greens and cook, stirring, until heated through and coated with the oil, about 5 minutes. Add the vinegar, red pepper flakes, and salt to taste. Remove from the heat.

When the polenta cake is ready, remove from the oven and invert onto a cutting board. Cut into wedges and divide among individual plates. Top the wedges with the warm greens, again dividing evenly, and scatter the cheese over the top. Serve immediately.

SERVES 8 TO 12

cont'd

Variations:

This versatile polenta cake also can be topped with the same cheese spread used with fried polenta (page 72), with herbed cream cheese and smoked salmon, with sautéed mushrooms and shaved Parmesan cheese, or with crab, shrimp, or smoked trout salad made with mayonnaise and celery.

WINE: The greens call for a wine that can handle strong flavors and a touch of spice, such as Montepulciano d'Abruzzo or Rosso Piceno or Rosso Conero from the Marche. For Montepulciano d'Abruzzo, look for producers such as Caldora, Masciarelli, or Farnese (be careful in your selection because there are Montepulciano d'Abruzzo jug wines, too). Velenosi and Pilastri are two great Rosso Piceno producers, and Moroder and Umani Ronchi are the preferred choices for Rosso Conero.

If you decide to make the smoked salmon or smoked trout variation, pour an aromatic white from Friuli or Alto Adige. Pinot Bianco (for its lemony flavors), Gewürztraminer (for its spice and intense aromatics), and Sylvaner (for its fresh acidity and aromatics) are three good choices. Abbazzia di Novacella, J. Hofstätter, Elena Walch, Colterenzio, Venica & Venica, and Schioppetto are reliable producers. If you opt for the crab or shrimp salad variation, Verdicchio and Falerio, both from the Marche, are good matches. The former boasts the flavors of almonds and stone fruits, while the latter is rounder and more aromatic. Bucci and Sartarelli are two excellent Verdicchio producers, while San Giovanni and Velenosi turn out the best Falerio.

Insalata di Riso Rice Salad

For the rice

1 cup short-grain Italian rice,
preferably Carnaroli

1½ cups water

1 teaspoon salt

For the vinaigrette

½ cup extra-virgin olive oil

¼ cup olive oil

¼ cup fresh lemon juice

3 tablespoons red wine vinegar

Salt and freshly ground black pepper

½ cup finely chopped red onion

¼ cup chopped fresh flat-leaf
parsley

cont'd

While Italian short-grain rice varieties do not hold up in a salad for as long as many long-grain types from elsewhere, such as basmati, Italian cooks use them in salads all the time and no one complains. As I noted earlier, I like to use Carnaroli because it has the largest grains of the commonly available Italian varieties. The key is not to let the salad sit for hours before serving. Garnishes can be folded in or arranged on top of the rice at serving time. *Insalata di riso alla marinara* calls for adding cooked clams, squid, and shrimp to the rice along with celery, olives, oil, garlic, vinegar, and marjoram. *Insalata di riso e peperoni arrostiti* is a simpler salad that includes roasted peppers, olives, oregano, capers, and garlic. I have suggested a number of additions here. Use as many or as few as you like.

o o o

To cook the rice, in a saucepan, combine the rice, water, and salt and bring to a boil over high heat. Cover, reduce the heat to low, and cook until the water is absorbed and the rice is tender, 15 to 18 minutes.

Meanwhile, make the vinaigrette: In a small bowl, whisk together the olive oils, lemon juice, and vinegar, and then whisk in salt and pepper to taste.

When the rice is ready, transfer it to a bowl. Drizzle with about ½ cup of the vinaigrette, toss well, and let cool. When the rice has cooled, fold in the onion and parsley and toss again. If you are adding the tuna, break it into large chunks with your fingers and toss in a bowl with about ¼ cup of the remaining vinaigrette. If you are adding the cooked shellfish instead, toss it with ¼ cup of the remaining vinaigrette.

cont'd

Suggested additions

1 can (7 ounces) olive oil-packed tuna, drained

1/2 pound cooked shellfish such as shrimp, clams, or squid (see Fish and Shellfish chapter for cooking techniques)

8 olive oil–packed anchovy fillets, drained and cut into narrow strips or chopped

2 red bell peppers, roasted, peeled, seeded, and cut lengthwise into narrow strips or coarsely diced

2 to 4 Preserved Artichokes (page 84), cut into quarters or eighths, depending on size

Pitted oil-cured black olives

Hard-boiled eggs, peeled and cut into wedges

Tomato wedges

At serving time, spoon a mound of rice onto each of 4 salad plates. Top with the dressed tuna or shellfish, anchovies, roasted peppers, artichokes, and/or olives, if using. Drizzle with the last of the vinaigrette (there should be about 6 tablespoons) and garnish with the egg and tomato wedges, if using. Or, mound the rice on a single large platter, top with your ingredients and garnishes of choice, and serve family style.

SERVES 4

WINE: Verdicchio dei Castelli di Jesi from the Marche, with its gorgeous flavors of almond and apple and its refreshing acidity, is a great marriage with this salad. A white blend from Sicily—Mirabile, Spadafora, and Donnafugata are good producers—would be a satisfying pairing, too.

Insalata di farro al profumo dell'orto
Wheat Salad with Garden Vegetables

For cooking the *farro*

2¹/₂ to 3 cups water

Salt

1 cup *farro*

¹/₂ cup extra-virgin olive oil, or more to taste

¹/₄ cup red wine vinegar, or more to taste

Salt and freshly ground black pepper

¹/₂ cup chopped red onion

¹/₂ cup chopped celery or fennel

¹/₂ cup peeled, chopped carrot

1 cup peeled, seeded, and chopped cucumber (see notes)

3 Preserved Artichokes (page 84), cut into wedges or diced (see notes)

4 small tomatoes, seeded and chopped (optional)

Grain salads lend themselves well to an antipasto assortment. For salads and soups, Pugliese cooks pound wheat berries to break the outer casing, arriving at a homemade version of cracked wheat (*grano pestato*). I prefer the sweeter, nuttier, and lighter textured *farro* found primarily in Tuscany and Abruzzo for my grain salads.

At the Locanda dell'Arte in Citta Sant'Angelo, in Abruzzo, the kitchen staff prepares a salad by cooking *farro* in vegetable broth, adding cooked artichokes, corn, cucumbers, mushrooms, peas, carrots, tomatoes, capers, and olives, and then garnishing with tuna. I am not a fan of using so many ingredients in a single salad, but I do agree that tuna, olives, and capers work well with a basic *farro* and vegetable salad, so here is my slimmed-down version.

ooo

To cook the *farro*, bring the water to a boil and salt it lightly. Add the *farro*, reduce the heat to low, cover, and simmer, checking for doneness after 20 to 25 minutes. When cooked the grain will be soft but still have some firmness at the center. If the *farro* is ready but not all the water has been absorbed, drain the cooked *farro* in a sieve. (Each brand absorbs water differently.) Place the drained *farro* in a bowl and let cool.

Add the ¹/₂ cup olive oil, ¹/₄ cup vinegar, and salt and pepper to taste to the cooled *farro* and toss to coat evenly. Then fold in the onion, celery, carrot, cucumber, artichokes, and the tomatoes, arugula, garlic, and chile, if using. Add the capers, parsley, and basil and taste and adjust the seasoning with more olive oil, vinegar, salt, and pepper.

Garnish the salad with olives, if desired. Serve at room temperature.

SERVES 8

Large handful of arugula leaves, tough stems removed and coarsely chopped (optional)

2 cloves garlic, finely minced (optional)

1 small fresh red chile, minced (optional)

2 tablespoons capers, rinsed and drained

1/4 cup chopped fresh flat-leaf parsley

1/4 cup chopped fresh basil or mint

Oil-cured black olives for garnish (optional)

NOTES: *For this salad, you can trim and cook the artichokes as directed for Preserved Artichokes (page 84, for short-term storage), let them cool, and then use them as they are, rather than preserving them in olive oil. Also, if you are using an English or Japanese cucumber, you do not need to peel it.*

WINE: Have one of the great whites from Campania, such as Falanghina, Greco di Tufo, or Fiano di Avellino. These are becoming easier to find outside of Italy, and there are a few exceptional producers. The most widely available is Feudi di San Gregorio, but also look for such up-and-coming labels as Villa Raiano, Vesevo, and De Conciliis.

Verdure
Vegetables

Traditional vegetable antipasti consist mainly of marinated vegetables, preserved *sott'olio* (in olive oil) or *sott'aceto* (in vinegar), cooked vegetables dressed with a simple vinaigrette or sauce, and cooked vegetables stuffed with rice, bread, or other fillings, served at room temperature. Contemporary chefs have added warm vegetable salads, room-temperature composed salads, and steamed vegetable puddings, or *sformati,* to this already bountiful mix, vastly expanding the repertoire.

I have slipped a classic Italian white bean salad (page 124) into the Fish and Shellfish chapter, as such salads are often paired with shellfish or tuna. Of course, you can make the bean salad without the seafood as a stand-alone vegetable antipasto or as part of an antipasto assortment. It also would be harmonious served with one of the eggplant or pepper salads or with *sott'olio* vegetables, or you can serve it topped with strips of prosciutto or salami or wedges of hard-boiled eggs.

Carciofi sott'olio Preserved Artichokes

1 lemon

6 large, 12 medium, or 24 small
artichokes

1 1/2 cups extra-virgin olive oil, or
as needed

1 cup fresh lemon juice

6 to 10 large, plump cloves garlic,
cut into slivers

4 small bay leaves

3 fresh thyme or marjoram sprigs

1 tablespoon kosher or sea salt

Antipasti Vegetables 84

Sott'olio, "in oil," is a way of preserving vegetables in olive oil for storage in the refrigerator or pantry. Here, I use this classic preparation for spring artichokes, which make a good contrast in an antipasto assortment that includes rich cured meats or fish, and also may be added to rice or *farro* salads (pages 77 and 80). *Sott'aceto,* another form of preservation, calls for vinegar rather than lemon juice with the oil and is closer to pickling (see variation). As a result, the vegetables are tarter and somewhat difficult to pair with wine.

o o o

Fill a bowl with cold water, halve the lemon, and squeeze the juice from each half into the water. Working with 1 artichoke at a time, remove almost all of the outer leaves until you reach tenderest pale green leaves. Pare away any dark green parts from the base and the stem. (If the stem does not seem fresh, cut it off flush with the base.) If using large artichokes, cut lengthwise into sixths; if using medium artichokes, cut lengthwise into quarters; and if using small artichokes, cut lengthwise into halves. With a small, sharp knife, cut away the choke (the chokes will probably not have formed yet in the small artichokes) and place the artichoke pieces in the lemon water. Repeat until all the artichokes are trimmed.

In a nonreactive pot, combine the 1 1/2 cups olive oil, lemon juice, garlic, herbs, and salt and bring to a simmer over medium heat. Drain the artichokes, add to the pot, and simmer, uncovered, until just cooked through but still firm, 10 to 15 minutes, for short-term shortage.

Remove from the heat, let cool, and transfer to a nonreactive container. Make sure the artichokes are immersed in the liquid. If not, add olive oil as needed to cover completely. Cover tightly and refrigerate for up to 2 weeks. Bring to room temperature to serve.

For long-term storage, sterilize a 1-quart canning jar and a two-part canning lid (self-sealing top and ring). Cook the artichokes for only 5 to 8 minutes. They should be barely translucent. Using tongs, transfer the artichokes to the sterilized jar and ladle the hot cooking liquid in to cover. Add additional olive oil as needed to cover the artichokes completely. Top the jar with the lid and screw on the metal ring.

Process in a hot-water bath for 20 minutes. Remove from the water bath and let cool completely. Make sure the jar has a good seal (the lid should be slightly indented in the center). Store in a cool, dark place for up to 6 months. If it failed to seal properly, store in the refrigerator for up to 2 weeks and bring to room temperature to serve.

SERVES 6 TO 8

Variation:

If you love pickled foods and are not serving wine, here is an excellent *sott'aceto* marinade for 3 pounds artichokes: Trim the artichokes as directed for the *sott'olio* marinade; leave whole if small or cut in half lengthwise if large. In a nonreactive pot, combine 4 cups white wine vinegar, 2 cups dry white wine, 6 cloves garlic, and 12 whole cloves and bring to a boil over high heat. Add the artichokes, reduce the heat to medium, and simmer, uncovered, until cooked through, 15 to 25 minutes, depending on size. Using a wire skimmer, transfer the artichokes to a dish towel to drain and discard the cooking liquid. Sterilize two 1-quart canning jars. Add a small rosemary sprig to each jar. Pour olive oil to a depth of 1 inch into the bottom of each jar. Using sterilized tongs, transfer about one-fourth of the artichokes to each jar, pushing down on them firmly to remove all air pockets. Add more olive oil and a sprinkling of red pepper flakes. Transfer the remaining artichokes to the jars, dividing them evenly and again pushing down on them to remove all air pockets. Add more oil as needed to cover the artichokes. Cover tightly and refrigerate for up to 2 months, or top each jar with a sterilized canning lid, screw on a metal ring, process in a hot-water bath for 15 minutes, and store in a cool, dark place for up to 6 months. You can use this same technique for 2 pounds bell peppers, quartered and seeded, or 3 pounds fresh button mushrooms, trimmed.

WINE: Pairing artichokes with wine is tricky. A wine that often works is Tocai Friulano, which can be a miracle for not only artichokes, but also for the equally challenging asparagus. Check out wines from Scarbolo, Bastianich, Movia, and Antico Broilo.

Involtini di melanzane Stuffed Eggplant Rolls

2 globe eggplants, peeled and sliced lengthwise 1/3 inch thick (18 to 20 slices)

1/2 cup extra-virgin olive oil, or as needed

Salt and freshly ground black pepper

For the stuffing

1/2 cup fine dried bread crumbs

1/2 cup grated pecorino or provolone cheese

1/4 cup chopped fresh flat-leaf parsley or equal parts parsley and basil

2 or 3 cloves garlic, finely minced

1 tablespoon grated lemon zest (optional)

Salt and freshly ground black pepper

Eggplant is incredibly versatile and thus widely popular at the antipasto table. These little rolls are among my favorite ways to serve it. If you grill the eggplant slices, they pick up a slight smokiness that adds a second layer of richness to the dish. If you don't want to fire up the grill, however, you can fry the eggplant slices. You can treat zucchini the same way, cutting it lengthwise into slices 1/3 inch thick and grilling or sautéing.

o o o

You can grill or fry the eggplant slices. To grill the slices, prepare a hot fire in a charcoal grill. When the fire is ready, brush the eggplant slices on both sides with the olive oil and sprinkle with salt and pepper. Place the eggplant slices directly over the fire and grill, turning once, until tender but not too soft, about 4 minutes total. Remove from the grill.

To fry the eggplant slices, place them in a colander, lightly salting the layers, and let stand for 30 minutes to drain. Pat the eggplant slices completely dry with paper towels. In a sauté pan, heat the olive oil over medium heat. Working in batches, add the eggplant slices and fry, turning once, until translucent and tender but not too soft, 6 to 8 minutes total. Transfer to paper towels to drain. Repeat with the remaining slices.

To make the stuffing, in a bowl, combine the bread crumbs, cheese, parsley, garlic, and the lemon zest, if using, and mix well. Season to taste with salt and pepper. (If you do not like the taste of raw garlic, sauté it in a little olive oil over low heat for a minute or two to tame its bite before combining it with the other ingredients.)

Preheat the oven to 400°F, or preheat the broiler.

Divide the bread crumb mixture evenly among the eggplant slices, spreading it evenly. Roll up the slices, and secure with toothpicks if they won't stay rolled. Lightly oil a baking dish (or a flameproof dish if using the broiler) large enough to accommodate the eggplant rolls in a single layer. Arrange the eggplant rolls, seam side down, in the dish. Drizzle the rolls with olive oil.

Place the dish in the oven or slip under the broiler about 4 inches from the heat source until the rolls are warmed through, just a few minutes in the broiler and 10 to 15 minutes in the oven.

Remove the toothpicks, if used, and arrange the rolls on a platter. Serve warm or at room temperature.

SERVES 4 TO 6

cont'd

Variations

Cook the eggplant slices as directed. In place of the bread-crumb mixture, dip strips of fresh mozzarella cheese in chopped fresh basil and roll up in the eggplant slices. Arrange the rolls in a baking dish, spoon a little tomato sauce (homemade without cream, page 42, or purchased) on top of each roll, or drizzle with olive oil, and bake in a 400°F oven just long enough to melt the cheese, about 15 minutes. Serve warm, while the cheese is still soft.

Prepare the eggplant slices as directed. In place of the bread-crumb mixture, roll up a slice of prosciutto, a strip of fresh mozzarella cheese, and a few whole fresh mint leaves in each eggplant slice. Arrange the rolls in a baking dish, drizzle with olive oil, and bake in a 400°F just long enough to melt the cheese, about 15 minutes. Serve warm, while the cheese is still soft.

Prepare the eggplant slices as directed. Make a thin egg omelet, cut into shapes to match the eggplant slices, and roll up the omelet pieces in the slices. Arrange the rolls in a baking dish, drizzle with tomato sauce (homemade without cream, page 42, or purchased), and bake in a 400°F oven for 10 to 15 minutes. Serve warm.

WINE: This is a wine-friendly antipasto. Both a Sangiovese and a Montepulciano work well with these flavors. Consider a juicy Morellino di Scansano from Tuscany's coast, a Rosso Conero from the Marche, or a Montefalco Rosso from Umbria.

Caponata Sicilian Sweet-and-Sour Eggplant

2 large globe eggplants, peeled, if desired, and cut into ³⁄₄-inch cubes

Salt

About 1¹⁄₂ cups extra-virgin olive oil

1 cup diced celery

3 yellow onions, sliced ¹⁄₄ inch thick

1 cup tomato purée

3 tablespoons capers, preferably salt packed, rinsed

15 to 20 pitted green olives, coarsely chopped

¹⁄₄ cup pine nuts, slivered blanched almonds, or pistachios, toasted

¹⁄₂ cup red wine vinegar

2 tablespoons sugar, or to taste

Freshly ground black pepper

This is one of the signature dishes of Sicily, symbolizing the exotic fusion characteristic of the island's cuisine: eggplant originated in Asia, the tomato is native to the New World, and the marriage of sweet and sour is borrowed from Arabic tradition. It is best made a day ahead of time and refrigerated to allow the flavors to marry. Bring to room temperature and taste and adjust the seasoning with more vinegar, salt, and sugar before serving. Serve in a bowl as a salad or spoon it on bruschette.

I am fussy about the quality of any red wine vinegar I use. Some vinegars are harsh and can detract from this dish. I prefer one made from Barolo or Barbaresco wine, or from good Cabernet. Select one that still has some wine flavor, along with the taste of the wood.

∘∘∘

Place the eggplants in a colander, lightly salting the layers, and let stand for 30 minutes to drain. Briefly rinse the eggplant cubes and pat completely dry with paper towels.

In a large, wide, deep sauté pan, heat a few tablespoons of the olive oil over medium heat. Add the celery and sauté until just beginning to soften, just a few minutes. It should still be crisp. Using a slotted spoon, transfer to a bowl and set aside.

Return the sauté pan to medium-high heat and add ¹⁄₂ cup of the olive oil. When the oil is hot, add half of the eggplant cubes and cook, turning often, until golden and cooked through, about 5 minutes. Using the slotted spoon, transfer to another bowl and set aside. Repeat with the remaining eggplant, adding oil as needed (probably ¹⁄₄ to ¹⁄₂ cup).

Return the sauté pan to medium heat. If the pan is dry, add a few tablespoons olive oil. Add the onions and sauté until soft but not brown, about 10 minutes. Add the celery and tomato purée and simmer for 10 minutes. Add the cooked eggplant, capers, olives, nuts, vinegar, and 2 tablespoons sugar and simmer for 20 minutes to blend the flavors. Season to taste with salt and pepper and with more sugar, if needed.

Remove from the heat and let cool. Serve at room temperature.

SERVES 8

WINE: A white or a red can be served here. For a white, choose one of the superb white blends from Sicily, such as Don Pietro Bianco from Spadafora. For a red, select a wine based on the Nero d'Avola grape, such as Cerasuolo di Vittoria, or look for a Nero d'Avola wine from COS, Planeta, Donnafugata, or Valle dell'Acate.

Peperonata con patate
Sweet Pepper and Potato Stew from Tuscany

1/2 cup extra-virgin olive oil

1 yellow onion, coarsely chopped

2 cloves garlic, finely minced

3 large red bell peppers, seeded and cut into 1/2-inch dice

2 large yellow or green bell peppers, seeded and cut into 1/2-inch dice

2 or 3 waxy potatoes such as Yukon gold, peeled and cut into 1/2-inch cubes

3 plum tomatoes, peeled, seeded, and diced (fresh or canned; about 1 cup)

Salt and freshly ground black pepper

2 to 3 tablespoons red wine vinegar

1/3 cup oil-cured black olives, pitted and halved (optional)

1/4 cup chopped fresh flat-leaf parsley or basil (optional)

In its most popular configuration, southern Italian *peperonata* combines strips of sautéed red and yellow peppers, onions, tomatoes, and sometimes a splash of vinegar. It can be made rather sweet with the addition of almonds and raisins. Some cooks add both sugar and vinegar for an *agrodolce,* or sweet-and-sour, taste. The Tuscan interpretation of this dish, like the Tuscans themselves, is sober and robust. It adds diced potatoes to the mixture, grounding it, and plays down the typical sweetness of the preparation. If you like, add some pitted olives for a briny accent.

o o o

In a large sauté pan, heat the olive oil over medium heat. Add the onion and sauté until soft, about 10 minutes. Add the garlic, bell peppers, potatoes, and tomatoes and mix well. Reduce the heat to low, cover, and cook until the potatoes and peppers are tender, about 30 minutes. Check the mixture from time to time and add a little water if it seems dry.

Season the mixture with salt and pepper. Add the vinegar and the olives, if using, and simmer for a few minutes to allow the flavors to mellow and mingle. Transfer to a serving dish and sprinkle with the parsley, if desired. Serve warm or at room temperature.

SERVES 8

WINE: When vegetables are prepared with vinegar, it can be a challenge to find a wine that works. But without fail, I am always happy with a glass of Franciacorta, Italy's answer to Champagne. Two other wines that complement this combination are Greco di Tufo from Campania and Verdicchio from the Marche.

Insalata di peperoni verdi Green Pepper Salad

1 pound green bell peppers (2 large)

2 to 3 tablespoons fresh
lemon juice

1/4 cup extra-virgin olive oil,
or more to taste

2 tablespoons chopped fresh
flat-leaf parsley

1 teaspoon dried oregano or
2 teaspoons chopped fresh marjoram
(optional)

Salt and freshly ground black pepper

Red and yellow peppers are sweet and can handle a dressing of wine vinegar easily. Green peppers are more assertive and have a sharper flavor, so with a salad of roasted green peppers I prefer to use lemon juice rather than vinegar, which can make them taste bitter. Don't be shy with the salt; it is crucial for balance. The salad can be made up to a day in advance, covered, and refrigerated; bring to room temperature before serving.

○ ○ ○

Sear the bell peppers over an open flame on a gas stove top or under the broiler until the skin is evenly charred on all sides and the peppers have softened. Place the peppers in a bowl, cover, and let steam for 15 minutes.

Remove the peppers from the bowl and scrape off the charred skin with a knife. Do not clean under running water, or you will lose much of the roasted flavor. Cut the peppers in half and remove the stems, seeds, and thick ribs. Cut each half lengthwise into strips 1/3 inch wide and transfer to a bowl.

In a small bowl, whisk together 2 tablespoons of the lemon juice and the olive oil. Whisk in the parsley and the oregano, if using. Season with salt and pepper, then taste and add more lemon juice, olive oil, salt, or pepper.

Drizzle the vinaigrette over the pepper strips, toss to mix, and serve at room temperature.

SERVES 4

WINE: Green peppers are difficult to pair with wine. Your best course of action is a white from Campania, such as Fiano di Avellino or Falaghina. Such wines are minerally and have ripe, aromatic fruits, making them a good match.

Funghi marinati Marinated Mushrooms

1/2 cup extra-virgin olive oil

2/3 cup red wine vinegar

2 cloves garlic, smashed

1 tablespoon sugar

1 teaspoon salt

1/4 cup water

1 small yellow onion, cut into 1/4-inch-thick rings

2/3 pound fresh small white button or cremini mushrooms

This is a family favorite. I served these mushrooms at my daughter's wedding, my son's birthday bash, and at many other celebrations. Why does everyone gobble them up? The answer is texture. The key here is not to marinate the mushrooms too long, so they still have some crunch. If you don't finish eating all of them, they will be good for days, of course, but will be softer. That's when you can throw them into a green salad. The leftover marinade can be added to your everyday vinaigrette.

o o o

In a deep bowl or crock, whisk together the olive oil, vinegar, garlic, sugar, salt, and water. Add the onion rings. Set aside.

Trim the stem ends on the mushrooms and then wipe the mushrooms clean with damp paper towels. Add to the marinade, stir gently to mix well, and leave at room temperature for 3 to 4 hours.

Serve the mushrooms with toothpicks for spearing.

SERVES 8

WINE: Because of the strong vinaigrette, you will want to pour a white wine, such as Falerio or Tocai Friulano. A sparkling wine would be good as well.

Insalata tiepida di funghi Warm Mushroom Salad

1/2 pound flavorful fresh mushrooms such as porcini, matsutake, chanterelle, or cremini

2 to 3 tablespoons olive oil

2 teaspoons minced garlic

Salt and freshly ground black pepper

4 large handfuls of young, tender salad greens (4 to 5 ounces total)

3 tablespoons extra-virgin olive oil

1 tablespoon aged balsamic vinegar

Shaved Parmesan cheese (optional)

In a perfect world, we all would be able to prepare this contemporary salad with fresh porcini, as they do at Il Desco restaurant in Verona. These sensual, costly mushrooms are not always at the market, nor can we always afford them when they are. But even penny-wise cremini will work here. The sautéed mushrooms make a wonderful topping for bruschette, too. You can also broil or grill portobello mushrooms, basting them with oil and balsamic vinegar and serve them warm atop a bed of greens. Trattoria dall'Amelia's Warm Salad of Scallops and Porcini on a bed of lettuces (page 130) showcases these prized mushrooms as well.

∘∘∘

Trim the stem ends on the mushrooms and then wipe the mushrooms clean with paper towels. If using porcini or matsutake, slice 1/8 inch thick. If using chanterelle or cremini, slice 1/4 inch thick.

In a large sauté pan, heat 2 tablespoons of the olive oil over medium heat. Add the mushrooms and garlic and sauté, adding more oil if the mushrooms begin to scorch, until the mushrooms are tender, about 5 minutes. Season with salt and pepper and remove from the heat.

Place the salad greens in a large bowl. In a small bowl, whisk together the extra-virgin olive oil and the vinegar and then whisk in salt and pepper to taste to make a vinaigrette.

Drizzle the vinaigrette over the salad greens and toss to coat evenly. Distribute the salad evenly among 4 salad plates. Top with the warm sautéed mushrooms, again dividing evenly. Scatter a few shavings of Parmesan cheese on top, if desired. Serve at once.

SERVES 4

WINE: This is a wine-friendly antipasto. My first instinct is to drink a Tocai Friulano. Other white options include Ribolla, Verdicchio, and Roero Arneis. If you want a red, consider a Lagrein, Barbera, Morellino di Scansano, or Rosso Conero.

Insalata di campo con bruciatini di prosciutto
Salad of Field Greens with Crunchy Prosciutto

For the salad

3/4 pound assorted salad greens, including arugula and radicchio, torn into bite-sized pieces

1/4 cup red wine vinegar

2 teaspoons Dijon mustard

About 3/4 cup extra-virgin olive oil

Salt and freshly ground black pepper

For the prosciutto

3 to 4 tablespoons extra-virgin olive oil

7 ounces sliced prosciutto, cut into strips about 1 1/2 inches long and 1/4 inch wide

2 tablespoons red wine vinegar

In the past, leafy salads were not considered a classic antipasto item. Today, you find them quite often, tossed or composed—a sign of the modern kitchen and French influence. A version of this salad is served as an antipasto at San Domenico di Imola, a celebrated restaurant in the history-rich town of Imola, in the province of Bologna. This fast and easy dish, which can be made with pancetta in place of the prosciutto, is also an ideal first course at a formal dinner.

o o o

To make the salad, place the salad greens in a large bowl. In a small bowl, whisk together the vinegar, mustard, and enough olive oil to make a balanced and flavorful vinaigrette. Season to taste with salt and pepper.

To cook the prosciutto, in a small sauté pan, heat the olive oil over high heat. Add the prosciutto strips and sauté, stirring to ensure even cooking, until they are a bit crunchy, 3 to 5 minutes. Using a slotted spoon, transfer the prosciutto to a plate. Add the vinegar to the pan and deglaze over high heat, scraping up any browned bits from the pan bottom, and then add to the vinaigrette.

Add the crisp prosciutto and the vinaigrette to the salad greens and toss well to combine. Serve immediately.

SERVES 4

WINE: Although it may be difficult to find, a dry Albana di Romagna from Emilia-Romagna, preferably a Tre Monti, would be wonderful with this salad. Most likely, you will need to look beyond Albana, however. Head to the neighboring Marche for a Verdicchio dei Castelli di Jesi, or across to the Piedmont for a minerally, ripe Gavi di Gavi.

I ripieni Stuffed Vegetables

For the rice stuffing

1/2 cup extra-virgin olive oil, plus oil for drizzling

1 yellow onion, chopped

1 cup Arborio rice

1 1/2 cups water

3 cloves garlic, finely chopped

1/4 cup chopped fresh flat-leaf parsley

1/4 cup fresh basil leaves, finely shredded

1 teaspoon salt

1/2 teaspoon freshly ground black pepper

For the bread crumb stuffing

4 slices coarse country bread, crusts removed, soaked in water, and squeezed almost dry

2 eggs, lightly beaten

3 tablespoons fine dried bread crumbs

cont'd

To be honest, these stuffed vegetables are a bit of work. The up side is that they can be prepared well ahead of time and make a truly impressive addition to the antipasto table. (Eat enough of them and you will have eaten dinner!) The vegetables may be served warm or at room temperature, just not dead cold. Select the savory stuffing of your choice: rice, bread crumb, or meat.

∘∘∘

Select a stuffing to make. To make the rice stuffing, in a large sauté pan, heat 1/4 cup of the olive oil over medium heat. Add the onion and sauté until soft, about 10 minutes. (If you are stuffing eggplants or zucchini, you will be sautéing the pulp from those vegetables at the same time.) Add the rice and sauté for 2 minutes longer, coating it well with the oil. Add the water and simmer, uncovered, until the water is absorbed, about 10 minutes. Remove from the heat and fold in the garlic, parsley, basil, and the remaining 1/4 cup olive oil. Season with the salt and pepper and mix again.

To make the bread crumb stuffing, in a bowl, combine the soaked bread, eggs, bread crumbs, cheese, garlic, parsley, and the mint, if using. Mix well, season with the salt and pepper, and mix again.

To make the meat stuffing, if using ground beef or sausage, heat the olive oil over medium-high heat. Add the beef or sausage meat and cook, stirring to break up any lumps, until it loses its red color, about 10 minutes. Remove from the heat and drain off the excess fat. If using roasted meat, chop the meat. In a bowl, combine the freshly cooked or roasted meat, bread crumbs, parsley, basil (if using), and garlic and mix well. Add the eggs, season with the salt and pepper, and mix again.

Select a vegetable to stuff. If using small tomatoes, cut a 1/2-inch-thick slice off the top of each tomato and reserve the caps. If using large tomatoes, cut in half crosswise. Using a small spoon or grapefruit spoon, a small serrated knife, or a melon baller, remove the pulp and juice, leaving a shell about 1/2 inch thick. If you have made the rice or meat stuffing, chop the pulp and add it to the stuffing; if you have made the bread crumb stuffing, reserve the pulp for another use. Sprinkle the cavity of each tomato case with a little salt and a pinch of sugar. Fill each about three-fourths full if using the rice stuffing (the rice will expand as the tomatoes cook); if using one of the other stuffings, you can fill more generously. Replace the caps if using small tomatoes.

cont'd

1/4 cup grated Parmesan cheese

3 cloves garlic, minced

2 tablespoons chopped fresh
flat-leaf parsley

2 tablespoons chopped fresh mint
(optional)

1 teaspoon salt

1/2 teaspoon freshly ground black
pepper

For the meat stuffing

2 tablespoons olive oil, if using
ground beef or sausage

1 pound ground beef; sweet Italian
sausages, casings removed; or
leftover roasted meat

1 cup fresh bread crumbs,
soaked in beef stock or water
and squeezed dry

1/4 cup chopped fresh flat-leaf
parsley

2 tablespoons chopped fresh basil,
mint, or marjoram (optional)

2 or 3 cloves garlic, minced

If using the bell peppers, cut a 1-inch-thick slice off the top of each pepper and reserve the caps. Remove and discard the seeds and ribs. Bring a large pot of water to a boil, add the peppers, and parboil for 4 to 5 minutes. Using tongs, lift the peppers out of the pot and invert to drain well. Fill each pepper about three-fourths full if using the rice stuffing (the rice will expand as the peppers cook); if using one of the other stuffings, you can fill more generously. Replace the caps.

If using the eggplants, cut each eggplant in half lengthwise. Using a small spoon or grapefruit spoon, a small serrated knife, or a melon baller, scoop out some of the pulp, leaving a shell about 1/2 inch thick. If using the rice stuffing, chop the pulp and sauté it with the onion in the olive oil until tender as directed in the first step of making the stuffing, and then finish the stuffing as directed. If making one of the other stuffings, reserve the pulp for another use. Film the bottom of a large sauté pan with olive oil and place over medium heat. Working in batches, add the eggplant cases and sauté, turning as needed, until softened, about 5 minutes. Fill each eggplant case about three-fourths full if using the rice stuffing (the rice will expand as the eggplants cook); if using one of the other stuffings, you can fill more generously.

If using the zucchini, cut each zucchini in half lengthwise. Using a small spoon or grapefruit spoon, a small serrated knife, or a melon baller, scoop out and discard the seeds from each half, and then scoop out some of the pulp, leaving a shell 1/4 to 1/3 inch thick. If using the rice stuffing, chop the pulp and sauté it with the onion in the olive oil until tender as directed in the first step of making the stuffing, and then finish the stuffing as directed. If making one of the other stuffings, reserve the pulp for another use or discard. Bring a large pot of water to a boil, add the zucchini cases, and parboil for 3 minutes. Using tongs, lift the zucchini cases out of the pot and invert to drain well. Fill each about three-fourths full if using the rice stuffing (the rice will expand as the zucchini cook); if using one of the other stuffings, you can fill more generously.

If using the onions, bring a large pot filled with water to a boil, add the onions, and boil until tender but not soft, about 10 minutes. Drain and, when cool enough to handle, cut in half crosswise. Using a small spoon or grapefruit spoon, a small serrated knife, or a melon baller, scoop out some of the pulp, leaving a shell 1/2 inch thick. If using the meat stuffing, chop the pulp and fold it into the stuffing. If making one of the other stuffings, reserve

2 eggs, lightly beaten

1 1/2 teaspoons salt

1/2 teaspoon freshly ground black pepper

For the vegetables (select one)

12 small or 6 large tomatoes

6 green bell peppers

6 small globe eggplants
(6 to 7 ounces each)

8 medium zucchini

6 large yellow onions

Salt and sugar, if using tomatoes

Extra-virgin olive oil as needed

the pulp for another use. Fill each onion case about three-fourths full if using the rice stuffing (the rice will expand as the onions cook); if using one of the other stuffings, you can fill more generously.

To bake the vegetables, preheat the oven to 375°F. Oil a baking dish large enough to hold the stuffed vegetables in a single layer without crowding. Place the vegetables in the dish and drizzle with olive oil. If you are baking tomatoes, add water to a depth of 1/2 inch to the baking dish. If the eggplant cases still seem quite firm, add the same amount of water to the dish.

Bake the vegetables until tender when pierced with a knife tip, 25 to 45 minutes (the tomatoes may take the longer amount of time because they have not been parboiled or fried in advance). Serve warm or at room temperature.

SERVES 12

WINE: Because there are so many diverse fillings and vegetables, the wine must work across a broad palette. For a white, a Verdicchio from the Marche is a crowd-pleaser and will pair well with the rice and bread stuffings. For a red, try a Rosso Conero, also from the Marche (but stay away from those labeled *riserva;* they are too big to complement antipasti). It has enough fruit balanced with great acidity to pair with all the fillings and vegetables. Moroder makes an excellent Rosso Conero.

Funghi ripieni al forno Baked Stuffed Mushrooms

Extra-virgin olive oil for preparing dish, sautéing, and drizzling

2 pounds fresh mushrooms, about 2 inches in diameter

2 cloves garlic, minced

2 tablespoons chopped fresh flat-leaf parsley

2 tablespoons chopped fresh marjoram

1/4 cup chopped prosciutto (optional)

2 slices coarse country bread, crusts removed, soaked in milk, and squeezed dry

1/2 cup grated Parmesan or *grana padano* cheese

2 eggs, lightly beaten

Salt and freshly ground black pepper

1/4 teaspoon freshly grated nutmeg

The Ligurian countryside is perfumed by a wonderful array of wild mushrooms. While your local store may not carry their equivalent, today a wide variety of mushrooms, both wild and cultivated, are generally available at better markets. This classic recipe works deliciously with everyday large cremini or white mushrooms.

ooo

Preheat the oven to 350°F. Oil a baking dish large enough to hold all of the mushrooms in a single layer without crowding.

Trim off the stems ends of the mushrooms and wipe the mushrooms clean with damp paper towels. Then carefully remove the stems and chop them finely. Set the caps and stems aside separately.

In a sauté pan, heat a few tablespoons olive oil over medium heat. Add the chopped stems, garlic, parsley, and marjoram and sauté, stirring often, until the mushroom pieces are tender and the flavors are blended, about 10 minutes. Transfer to a bowl and add the prosciutto (if using), soaked bread, cheese, eggs, and 1 or 2 tablespoons olive oil so that the filling is moist but not too wet. Mix well, distributing all the ingredients evenly, and then season with 1 teaspoon salt, 1/2 teaspoon pepper, and the nutmeg and mix well again.

Spoon a heaping spoonful of the filling into each mushroom cap, mounding it nicely, and arrange the filled mushrooms in the prepared dish. Sprinkle them with salt and pepper and drizzle with olive oil. Pour water to a depth of about 1/3 inch into the baking dish (see note).

Bake the mushrooms until they are tender and the stuffing is golden, 35 to 40 minutes. Serve immediately.

SERVES 6

NOTE: *If you don't want to add water to the baking dish for fear of losing mushroom flavor to the dish juices, sauté the mushroom caps briefly in butter or olive oil to soften them, and then fill and bake as directed.*

WINE: Many wines complement the earthiness of mushrooms. For this preparation, choose a wine that is not too big or tannic. On the white side, select a Vermentino, Roero Arneis, Gavi di Gavi, Tocai Friulano, or Pinot Bianco. For a red wine, look to a young Barbera d'Alba, a Chianti, or a Sangiovese from the Maremma, Tuscany's southwest coast.

Pomodori farciti al formaggio squaquarone e basilico
Tomatoes Filled with Creamy Cheese and Basil

4 tomatoes, about 3 inches in diameter

Salt

2 ounces slender green beans, ends trimmed

3 ounces cottage cheese or *fromage blanc* or other moist, soft fresh cheese (see recipe introduction)

¼ cup heavy cream, sour cream, or quark, or as needed

¼ cup fresh basil leaves, cut into narrow strips

Salt and freshly ground black pepper

Lettuce leaves (optional)

Extra-virgin olive oil

Squaquarone is a very soft cow's milk cheese from Emilia-Romagna. It is not exported, so for this recipe you will have to improvise, using ricotta, *fromage blanc,* cottage cheese, or farmer cheese and enriching it with heavy cream, quark, or sour cream. What is important is that the cheese mixture be soft and creamy. This salad, like the salad with prosciutto on page 95, is served at the lovely San Domenico di Imola restaurant. I am a bit of a classicist, so I find the restaurant's presentation—green beans sticking out of the top of the tomato like porcupine quills, random raw onion rings strewn on top, and lettuce leaves leaning on the side—a bit fussy. The tomatoes filled with green beans and cheese are perfect antipasto fare, however. At my table, I skip the embellishment, but you can go as baroque as you like. Don't bother to make this dish unless your tomatoes are ripe but firm and flavorful.

○○○

Bring a saucepan filled with water to a boil. Using a sharp knife, cut a shallow X in the blossom end of each tomato. When the water is boiling, slip 2 of the tomatoes into the water and leave for 20 to 30 seconds to loosen the skins. Lift out the tomatoes with a slotted spoon and immerse in a bowl of cold water. Repeat with the remaining 2 tomatoes. Drain the tomatoes and, beginning at the X, carefully peel away the skin. Then, cut a ½-inch-thick slice off the stem end of each tomato; reserve the caps to use a garnish, if desired.

Using a small spoon or grapefruit spoon, a small serrated knife, or a melon baller, remove the center of each tomato, leaving a shell about ⅓ inch thick. Save the pulp for another use or discard. Sprinkle the inside of each tomato with a little salt. Invert the tomatoes in a colander and leave to drain for 10 minutes.

Fill the saucepan with fresh water, bring to a boil, and salt lightly. Add the green beans and cook until tender-crisp, 2 to 3 minutes. Drain and refresh in a bowl filled with ice water. When cold, drain again and pat dry. Cut crosswise into 1-inch pieces.

cont'd

Tomatoes Filled with Creamy Cheese and Basil   cont'd

In a bowl, combine the cheese and 1/4 cup cream and mix well. The mixture should be spoonable and have the consistency of a very soft cottage cheese; if it is not, add a little more cream. Using a spatula, fold in the green beans and basil. Season to taste with salt and pepper.

If using lettuce leaves, line 4 salad plates with them. Spoon the cheese mixture into the tomatoes, dividing it evenly. Place the tomatoes on the plates, drizzle the top of each tomato with a little olive oil, and lean a tomato cap alongside each tomato, if you like. Serve at room temperature.

SERVES 4

WINE: You want a wine that will dance with the rich, creamy cheese, the acid from tomatoes, and the crunch from the green beans. A Greco di Tufo will capture the aromatics and the mineral accents. Look for one from Mastroberardino, Vesevo, Feudi di San Gregorio, or Villa Raiano.

Fagiolini alle nocciole Green Beans with Hazelnuts

Salt

1 pound slender green beans, trimmed

Juice of 2 lemons (about $1/2$ cup)

3 shallots, finely minced

$2/3$ cup heavy cream

2 tablespoons hazelnut oil (optional)

Freshly ground black pepper

Butter lettuce leaves (optional)

4 figs, cut into quarters through the stem end (optional)

$3/4$ cup hazelnuts, toasted, peeled, and coarsely chopped

Here is yet another memorable dish from the famed San Domenico di Imola restaurant. For this one, chef Valentino Marcattilii serves slim French haricots verts with a cream-enriched hazelnut dressing. While he offers this as a composed salad on individual plates, the beans arranged over tender hearts of lettuce, you may opt for a simpler platter presentation without the greens. If figs are in season, they are a lovely addition to the salad. I have added hazelnut oil to the dressing, as I like the richness and the contrast to the grassiness of the beans that it contributes.

o o o

Bring a large saucepan filled with water to a boil and salt the water lightly. Add the beans and cook until tender-crisp, 2 to 3 minutes. Drain and refresh in a bowl filled with ice water. When cold, drain again and pat dry. Place in a bowl.

In a small bowl, whisk together the lemon juice, shallots, cream, and the hazelnut oil, if using. Season to taste with salt and pepper.

If using lettuce leaves, arrange them on a platter or individual plates. Drizzle the creamy dressing over the beans and toss to coat evenly. Place the beans on top of the lettuce leaves, or on a single platter or individual plates. Surround with the figs, if using. Sprinkle with the hazelnuts and serve immediately.

SERVES 4

Variations: You can use toasted walnuts in place of the hazelnuts and walnut oil in place of the hazelnut oil. Also, using grilled, rather than raw, figs adds an additional layer of flavor.

WINE: Tocai Friulano, always a great match with hazelnuts, is ideal here, but the citrus profile and aromatics of Sauvignon Blanc would work nicely, too, especially with the green beans. A Pinot Bianco is yet another choice. It is less intense than a Sauvignon Blanc and would please everyone with its freshness and drinkability. If the figs are used, Tocai will be the best match; the Sauvignon Blanc may clash with their sweetness. Among the top Tocai producers are Schioppetto, Borgo Tesis, Bastianich, and Movia.

Asparagi al forno e fonduta
Roasted Asparagus and Creamy Cheese Sauce

For the *fonduta*

7 ounces Fontina cheese from Valle d'Aosta, cut into small dice

Whole milk to cover

2 tablespoons unsalted butter

2 egg yolks, lightly beaten

Salt and freshly ground black pepper

Truffle oil, truffle paste (see note, page 41), or shaved fresh truffle (optional)

2 pounds asparagus

3 tablespoons extra-virgin olive oil

Salt and freshly ground black pepper

When asparagus is in season, I want to eat it every day. Many cooks steam the spears, but roasting gives them a satisfying earthy flavor. Or, you can parboil the asparagus and then put them on a grill for a minute or two to give them a hint of smokiness. The *fonduta,* a specialty of northern Italy, can also be served with bread sticks for dipping. Be sure to seek out the delicately nutty, straw-colored Fontina made in the Italian Alps. If you are using the optional truffle (in any form), white is preferred, though black can be used.

o o o

Preheat the oven to 450°F.

To make the *fonduta,* in a bowl, combine the cheese and milk, cover, and let rest in the refrigerator for 4 hours. The cheese will absorb some of the milk.

Snap off the tough ends of the asparagus spears, and then trim the ends so they are even. If the spears are very thick, peel the bottom half with a vegetable peeler. Pour the olive oil into a shallow bowl large enough to accommodate the length of the spears, and roll the spears in the oil. Arrange the spears in a single layer on a rimmed baking sheet, allowing a little space between them. Sprinkle with salt and pepper.

Place the asparagus in the oven and roast until tender, 7 to 10 minutes; the timing will depend on the thickness of the spears.

Meanwhile, to finish the *fonduta,* melt the butter in the top of a double boiler over simmering water. Add the cheese and milk and stir in the egg yolks. Cook gently, stirring often, until the cheese is melted and creamy, about 10 minutes. Season with salt and pepper and stir in the truffle oil, if you like it.

Remove the asparagus from the oven and arrange on individual plates. Spoon the *fonduta* over the tips and serve immediately.

SERVES 6

Variations: Instead of roasting the asparagus spears, you can sauté them in 3 tablespoons unsalted butter in a nonstick pan over low heat, turning them often, until they are lightly browned and tender, about 8 minutes. You can also forgo the *fonduta.* Top the asparagus with grated Parmesan cheese in its place.

WINE: Asparagus is often a tough match with wine, but fortunately the Italians have some wines that will work here. Tocai Friulano is one. You can also try a white blend from Friuli. Look for wines from the Collio, Colli Orientali, Grave, or Isonzo appellation and from such producers as Movia, Venica & Venica, Schioppetto, and Scarbolo.

Sformato di cavolfiore Cauliflower Pudding

Salt

1 large head cauliflower, trimmed and divided into florets (4 to 5 cups)

1 lemon zest strip (optional)

Unsalted butter for preparing mold(s), plus 4 tablespoons

1¼ cups whole milk or half-and-half

¼ cup all-purpose flour

Freshly ground black pepper

Freshly grated nutmeg

Pinch of cayenne pepper (optional)

3 eggs, lightly beaten

½ cup grated Parmesan cheese

Sformati are flans or custards that are unmolded (*sformare*) onto a plate. They are reminiscent of French cooking and are popular antipasti in the Piedmont, where Gallic cuisine has a history. Some *sformati* are sauced with *fonduta* (page 105), while others are treated to a light tomato sauce or a purée of roasted red peppers thinned with cream. Here I have included a seafood sauce, but you can omit it and still have a wonderful dish, or you can make a tomato sauce or pepper sauce; plan on about 1½ cups. *Sformati* custards are rich, so you need to keep the portions small. This same basic method can be used for other vegetables (see variations).

Contemporary chefs regularly build on these traditional custards. For example, superstar chef Gianfranco Vissani, a popular television personality and the genius behind Rome's celebrated Casina Valadier, has created a modern spinach *sformato* in a Parmesan-scented broth with sautéed chicken livers and diced croutons.

∘∘∘

Bring a large saucepan filled with water to a boil. Lightly salt the water, add the cauliflower and the lemon zest strip (if you want to reduce the strong cabbagey smell), and cook until very tender, about 20 minutes.

Meanwhile, preheat the oven to 350°F. Butter a 1½-quart soufflé dish or other round baking dish or eight ¾-cup custard cups. Place the dish or cups in a large baking pan.

When the cauliflower is ready, drain well, transfer to a food processor, and purée until smooth. Transfer to a bowl. (If the purée seems quite wet, spoon it into a sieve placed over a bowl and set aside to drain for about 1 hour, then transfer to a bowl.) You should have 2½ to 3 cups purée.

In a small saucepan, warm the milk over medium heat until small bubbles appear around the edge of the pan, then remove from the heat. At the same time, in another saucepan, melt the 4 tablespoons butter over medium heat. When the foam subsides, add the flour and whisk until smooth. Reduce the heat to low and cook, stirring constantly, for 5 minutes; do not allow the mixture to color. Gradually add the hot milk while whisking constantly, then continue to cook, stirring often, until the mixture thickly coats the back of a spoon, 3 to 5 minutes. Season to taste with salt and black pepper and with a generous amount of nutmeg. Add the cayenne if you want a bit of heat.

For the optional seafood sauce

3 tablespoons unsalted butter

¼ pound fresh-cooked crabmeat
or baby shrimp

½ cup dry white wine

¼ cup heavy cream

Salt and freshly ground black pepper

1 tomato, peeled, seeded, and diced
(optional)

2 tablespoons chopped fresh chives
or flat-leaf parsley

Add the white sauce to the cauliflower purée, and then stir in the eggs and cheese.

Pour the mixture into the prepared mold(s) and add hot water to the baking pan to reach halfway up the sides of the mold(s). Cover the pan with aluminum foil.

Bake the custard(s) until set when tested with a thin knife blade, 50 to 60 minutes for a single large one and 25 to 30 minutes for the small ones. Remove the mold(s) from the water bath and let rest for 10 minutes.

Meanwhile, make the seafood sauce, if using: In a sauté pan, melt the butter over medium heat. Add the crabmeat and wine and heat through for a minute or two to cook off some of the alcohol. Add the cream, season with salt and pepper, and then stir in the tomato, if using (if you don't have a ripe, flavorful in-season tomato, don't use it), and the chives and again heat through. Remove from the heat and keep hot.

Run a knife around the inside edge of the baking dish to loosen the sides of the custard, invert a serving plate over the dish, and invert the plate and dish together. Lift off the dish. Or, loosen the small custards and invert onto individual plates. Spoon the sauce around the edges. Serve immediately.

SERVES 8

Variations: You can substitute a variety of other vegetables for the cauliflower: 2 pounds zucchini, carrots, mushrooms, butternut squash, or spinach or 6 large artichoke hearts. Once they are cooked and puréed, or finely chopped in the case of the spinach, each will yield 2½ to 3 cups. If you are using butternut squash, purée the squash with 1 tablespoon chopped fresh sage. You can serve *fonduta* (page 105) or Tomato Sauce (page 42, made with cream) with any of the suggested variations or with the cauliflower custard. You can serve the seafood sauce with the spinach or artichoke variation.

WINE: You need to choose a wine that will deliver some balance to the richness of the custard. A flinty Verdicchio would be delicious, as would whites from the Alto Adige, including Pinot Bianco, Kerner, Veltliner, and Pinot Grigio. Look for such producers as J. Hofstätter, Alois Lageder, St. Michael-Eppan, Elena Walch, and Terlano.

Pesce e frutti di mare
Fish and Shellfish

As you can see by the number of recipes in this chapter, fish and shellfish are a source of creative inspiration for chefs and home cooks alike. In Shop-and-Serve Antipasti, I have talked about the simplest raw fish dishes—*crudo,* carpaccio, tartare—and the easily assembled smoked fish plates. In this chapter, you will find both classic and contemporary recipes for marinated fish, cooked fish and shellfish with vegetables or beans, and warm and cold seafood salads. Any one of these will add drama to an antipasto assortment or can star as a course on its own.

Insalata di mare Seafood Salad

Salt

1/2 pound medium shrimp, peeled and deveined

3/4 pound squid, cleaned, bodies cut into 1/2-inch-wide rings, and tentacles left whole if small or halved if large (or 1/2 pound cleaned squid)

2 pounds clams, well scrubbed

2 pounds mussels, beards removed and well scrubbed

1/2 cup dry white wine or water

1/2 cup extra-virgin olive oil

3 tablespoons fresh lemon juice, or more to taste

1 or 2 tablespoons fresh orange juice (optional)

Freshly ground black pepper

1/4 to 1/2 teaspoon red pepper flakes

6 to 8 celery stalks, cut crosswise on the diagonal into narrow strips

The ancient Romans loved celery and ascribed aphrodisiacal properties to it. I cannot make any promises of romantic conquests, but celery does offer a clean and crunchy contrast to the richness of the shellfish. A citrus vinaigrette, rather than a vinegar one, is best if you plan to serve this with wine. Piedmontese chef Cesare Giaccone adds a squeeze of orange juice and a few drops of slightly sweet and mild Moscato vinegar of his own production to the basic lemon and olive oil dressing. This classic salad can be part of an antipasto assortment or served solo, with or without a bed of lettuce leaves.

∘∘∘

Bring a small saucepan filled with water to a boil over high heat. Lightly salt the water, add the shrimp, reduce the heat to medium, and simmer for 2 minutes. Add the squid and simmer for 1 1/2 to 2 minutes longer. At this point, both should be just cooked, with the shrimp pink and the squid opaque. Using a wire skimmer, lift out the shrimp and squid and refresh in a bowl of ice water. When cool, drain well, place in a bowl, and set aside.

In a large saucepan, combine the clams, mussels, and wine, cover, and place over medium-high heat. After a few minutes, uncover and remove any mussels or clams that have opened and place in a bowl. Re-cover and continue cooking until all the mollusks have surrendered to the steam. This should take no more than 7 minutes (the mussels will open more quickly, usually 3 to 4 minutes sooner than the clams, which can be stubborn). Discard any mollusks that failed to open. When cool enough to handle, remove the clams and mussels from their shells, add them to the shrimp and squid, and discard the shells. You can strain the cooking liquid through a cheesecloth-lined sieve and reserve it for another use, or you can discard it.

In a small bowl, whisk together the olive oil, the lemon juice to taste, and the orange juice to taste, if using, and then season lightly with salt and black pepper to make a vinaigrette. Clams are a bit salty, so you don't want to add too much salt now. Add 1/4 teaspoon red pepper flakes, and wait to add more later to taste, so that the salad will not be too spicy.

1 red bell pepper, seeded and cut lengthwise into narrow strips or diced (optional)

2 tablespoons chopped fresh flat-leaf parsley

Add the celery and bell pepper (if using) to the shellfish, drizzle with the vinaigrette, and toss to coat evenly. Taste and adjust the seasoning with salt, black pepper, and red pepper flakes. Spoon onto individual plates or a single platter and sprinkle with the parsley. Serve at room temperature.

SERVES 4

WINE: Vermentino from Sardinia or Liguria is an excellent choice for this salad. Top producers from Sardinia include Contini, Cantina Sociale Gallura, and Argiolas, and from Liguria, Enoteca Bisson, Fratelli Parma, and Colle dei Bardellini.

Insalata di frutti di mare, arancie e finocchio
Shellfish Salad with Oranges and Fennel

For the vinaigrette

1 cup extra-virgin olive oil

$1/2$ cup fresh orange juice

$1/4$ cup fresh lemon juice

1 tablespoon freshly ground coarse black pepper

Salt

3 navel oranges

2 or 3 fennel bulbs, cored, trimmed, and thinly sliced lengthwise

2 cups dry white wine or equal parts wine and water

18 medium shrimp, peeled and deveined

18 sea scallops, foot muscle removed

12 small squid, cleaned, bodies cut into narrow rings, and tentacles left whole

Chopped fresh flat-leaf parsley or fennel leaves for garnish

Orange paired with anise-scented fennel is a traditional Sicilian flavor marriage. This recipe takes the combination one step further with the addition of shellfish. Contemporary chefs like to serve the shellfish warm, in contrast to the cool orange and fennel salad. If time permits, you may want to warm the seafood briefly. Here, instead of using red pepper flakes, I add the subtler heat of black pepper to the vinaigrette. If you like, you can use red pepper flakes for some of the black pepper. Thinly sliced celery is a nice alternative if your market does not have fennel.

ooo

To make the vinaigrette, in a small bowl, whisk together the olive oil and the citrus juices. Whisk in the pepper and the salt to taste. Set aside.

Working with 1 orange at a time, cut a thin slice off the top and bottom to reveal the flesh. Stand the orange upright and remove the peel in wide strips, cutting downward and following the contour of the fruit. Holding the orange over a bowl, cut along both sides of each segment, releasing the segments from the membrane and allowing them to drop into the bowl. Using the knife tip, pry out any seeds from the segments. Squeeze the membrane over the bowl to collect extra juice that you can add to the vinaigrette at serving time.

Place the fennel in a bowl, add half of the vinaigrette, and toss to coat evenly. Divide the fennel evenly among 8 salad plates, forming a bed on each one, or arrange the fennel in a bed on a large platter.

cont'd

In a saucepan, bring the wine to a simmer over medium heat. Add the shrimp and cook gently until they turn pink and are cooked through, about 4 minutes. Do not overcook or they will be tough. Using a slotted spoon, transfer the shrimp to a bowl. Add the scallops to the pan and simmer gently until just opaque throughout, about 2 minutes. Transfer with the slotted spoon to the bowl holding the shrimp. Add the squid to the pan and cook until they turn opaque, about 1 minute. Scoop out with the slotted spoon and add to the shrimp and scallops. Drizzle about one-third of the remaining vinaigrette over the seafood and toss to coat evenly.

Using the slotted spoon, remove the orange segments from the bowl and distribute evenly over the fennel. Then distribute the warm seafood evenly over the fennel. Add the orange juice from the bowl to taste to the remaining vinaigrette and drizzle the vinaigrette over the salad. Top with the parsley. Serve warm or at room temperature.

SERVES 8

WINE: Sicilian white wines have sufficient body and texture to balance the flavors of fennel and citrus beautifully. Stay away from Chardonnay and try the local blends from producers such as Donnafugata, Mirabile, Planeta, and Spadafora.

Insalata di aragosta al pesto Lobster Salad with Pesto

For the pesto

1 cup firmly packed fresh basil leaves

1 teaspoon finely minced garlic

2 tablespoons pine nuts or walnuts, toasted

1/2 cup extra-virgin olive oil

1/2 teaspoon salt

1/2 teaspoon freshly ground black pepper

12 to 18 small new potatoes (number depends on size)

Salt

1/2 pound small, slender green beans, trimmed

3 small lobsters, about 11/4 pounds each (about 1 pound meat total)

1/4 cup white wine vinegar

About 1/4 cup extra-virgin olive oil

Salt and freshly ground black pepper

Tiny cherry tomatoes for garnish (optional)

In Liguria, potatoes, green beans, and pesto form a popular trio for tossing with pasta. Here, that same mix is used in an elegant seafood salad. Lobster, of course, takes this combination to another level, but you don't have to splurge on lobster every time you want to make this wonderful dish. You can substitute cooked shrimp, scallops, mussels, or use a combination of shellfish. And you can be as thrifty as late chef Angelo Paracucchi, of the famed Locanda dell'Angelo restaurant near the medieval town of Ameglia, in Liguria. He sometimes used a pound of cooked fish fillet instead of the lobster.

∘∘∘

To make the pesto, in a food processor, combine the basil leaves, garlic, and nuts and pulse a few times to combine. Add the 1/2 cup olive oil and process until you have a coarse purée. (The balance of the olive oil will be added later.) Season with the salt and pepper. Set aside.

In a saucepan, combine the potatoes with water to cover, add a little salt, and bring to a boil over high heat. Reduce the heat to medium and simmer until the potatoes are cooked through but still firm. The cooking time will vary with the size of the potatoes, but very small ones will cook in about 10 minutes or so and larger ones in about 15 minutes or longer. When done, drain well and let cool to room temperature.

Meanwhile, bring a second saucepan filled with water to a boil over high heat. Lightly salt the water and then add the green beans and cook until tender-crisp, 2 to 3 minutes. Drain and refresh in a bowl filled with ice water. When cold, drain again and pat dry.

Bring a large pot of water to a boil over high heat. Salt the water liberally and add the lobsters. Cover, reduce the heat to low, and cook until they turn red, about 9 minutes. (If you have been able to find only 1-pound lobsters, cook them for about 7 minutes; if you are using 11/2-pound lobsters, cook for about 11 minutes. Or, you can steam the lobsters on a rack over boiling water for a particularly tender result; allow 10 minutes for 1-pound lobsters, 12 minutes for 11/4-pound lobsters, and 14 minutes for 11/2-pound lobsters.)

cont'd

When the lobsters are ready, transfer them to a sink filled with ice water and leave until cold. Then, working with 1 lobster at a time, twist off the tail section from each body. Cut through the tail shell, pry it open to reveal the meat, lift out the meat, and discard the black vein down the center. Cut the tail meat into medallions. Crack the claws and extract the meat, leaving the pieces whole for a showy presentation, if desired. Refrigerate the lobster meat until needed.

Transfer the pesto to a bowl and stir in the vinegar and add enough of the 1/4 cup olive oil to make a spoonable vinaigrette. Season to taste with salt and pepper.

To serve, cut the potatoes into 1/4-inch-thick slices or into halves if they are very small.

In a bowl, combine the potatoes, green beans, and about 1/2 cup of the vinaigrette and toss to coat evenly. Distribute the potato mixture evenly among salad plates. Top with the lobster, again dividing evenly, and drizzle with the remaining vinaigrette. Garnish with tiny cherry tomatoes, if desired. Serve immediately.

SERVES 6 TO 8

Variations: You can substitute 1 pound large shrimp, peeled and deveined, or sea scallops, foot muscle removed, for the lobsters. Pour dry white wine or water to a depth of 2 inches into a wide saucepan and bring to a boil over high heat. If you are using water, lightly salt it. If you are using shrimp, add them to the pan, reduce the heat to medium, and cook until they turn pink, 3 to 4 minutes. If using scallops, add them to the pan, reduce the heat to medium, and cook until they are just opaque throughout, about 2 minutes. Drain, refresh in ice water, and refrigerate until serving. Or, you can cook them just before serving and serve them warm.

WINE: In Liguria, the key white grapes are Vermentino, Pigato, and Bianchetta Genovese, but far too many of the great wines made from them never make it to our shores. Look for wines that are lemony, flinty, and minerally from Enoteca Bisson, Fratelli Parma, or Colle dei Bardellini. If you cannot find Ligurian wines, seek out wines from Sardinia from producers such as Contini and Argiolas. Or, perhaps try the richer-styled Tuscan Tenuta Guado al Tasso Vermentino from Antinori. Another option is a *rosato* from Sardinia.

Insalata di calamari e carciofi Squid and Artichoke Salad

1 lemon, plus 4 tablespoons fresh lemon juice

2 large or 3 medium artichokes

1/4 cup plus 6 tablespoons extra-virgin olive oil

6 cups water

3 tablespoons white wine vinegar

1 fresh thyme sprig

1/2 bay leaf

5 black peppercorns, bruised

1 pound small squid, cleaned and bodies and tentacles left whole

1 small fennel bulb, trimmed, cored, and cut lengthwise into narrow strips

1/2 large or 1 very small cucumber, preferably Japanese, peeled, halved lengthwise, seeded, and cut into narrow strips

You want the smallest, most tender squid for this dish, preferably no more than 2 1/2 to 3 inches long. If you can find only larger squid, cut them crosswise into rings about 1/3 inch wide, cut the tentacles in half, and cook for only 2 minutes. If your market is out of squid, you can use shrimp instead.

In Italy, artichokes are often served raw, thinly sliced. Alas, ours are stored longer at the market and are tougher, plus they have a particularly wiry choke. Because of this, I usually cook artichoke hearts for salad. If you can find very fresh, very tender baby artichokes, slice them paper-thin on a mandoline (use the hand guard!) at the very last minute; as you cut them, slip the slices into water mixed with a little lemon juice to keep them from discoloring; and then drain, pat dry, and add them to the salad.

If you want to serve wine, and find artichokes an impossible match, follow the example of Lombardian-based chef Gualtiero Marchesi and use tiny green beans instead. And if you have any salad left over, chop it coarsely, warm it, and serve it atop bruschette, as they do at Ristorante Oca Bianca, just outside the Tuscan beach town of Viareggio.

Fill a bowl with cold water, halve the lemon, and squeeze the juice from each half into the water. Working with 1 artichoke at a time, remove all the leaves until you reach the tenderest pale green leaves. Pare away any dark green parts from the base and the stem. (If the stem does not seem fresh, cut it off flush with the base.) Cut the artichoke in half lengthwise and, using a sharp-edged spoon or a melon baller, remove and discard the choke from each half. Cut each half lengthwise into 1/4-inch-thick slices and place the slices in the lemon water. Repeat until all the artichokes are trimmed.

Drain the artichoke slices. In a sauté pan, warm the 1/4 cup olive oil over low heat. Add the artichokes, 1 tablespoon of the lemon juice, and just enough water to cover the artichokes. Simmer, stirring occasionally, until the artichoke slices are cooked through (they will be translucent) but not too soft and most of the water has evaporated, 10 to 15 minutes. Remove from the heat and let cool in the pan.

In a saucepan, combine the water, vinegar, thyme, bay and peppercorns and bring to a boil over high heat. Add the squid, reduce the heat to medium, and cook just until opaque, about 4 minutes. Drain well and let cool.

o o o

1 teaspoon salt, or to taste

Freshly ground black pepper

3 tablespoons chopped fresh
flat-leaf parsley

3 tablespoons chopped fresh mint

Drain the cooled artichokes. In a salad bowl, combine the fennel, cucumber, and artichokes. In a small bowl, whisk together the remaining 6 tablespoons olive oil and the remaining 3 tablespoons lemon juice, and then whisk in the salt and the pepper to taste to make a vinaigrette.

Add the squid to the vegetables and drizzle with the vinaigrette. Toss to coat evenly and then sprinkle with the parsley and mint. Serve at room temperature.

SERVES 6

WINE: Open a Prosecco, or pour a Franciacorta, Italy's first-rate answer to Champagne. Look for Prosecco from Bisol, Collalbrigo, Dea, Drusian, Fantinel, or Sorelle Bronca. Or, try a Verdicchio from such Marche producers as Bucci and Sartarelli.

Gamberi alla crema di piselli Shrimp with Pea Purée

3 cups water

Salt

1 pound English peas, shelled
(about 1 cup shelled)

4 tablespoons extra-virgin olive oil,
plus oil for drizzling

Freshly ground black pepper

All-purpose flour for dusting

16 medium to large shrimp (about
3/4 pound), peeled and deveined

1 clove garlic, minced

1/2 cup dry white wine

Chopped fresh flat-leaf parsley
for garnish

This contemporary dish, served at Vineria Cozzi in Bergamo Alto, is a knockout! Not only is it delicately delicious, with the sweetness of shrimp playing against the sweetness of spring peas, but it is also a beautiful plate, with the pink shellfish resting in a sea of pale green. As an alternative, you can serve the shrimp with an asparagus purée.

◦ ◦ ◦

In a saucepan, bring the water to a boil over high heat. Lightly salt the water, add the peas, reduce the heat to medium, and simmer until tender, 3 to 7 minutes, depending on the size and starchiness of the peas. (If peas are not in season or the fresh ones taste too starchy, you can use 1 cup frozen peas.) Remove from the heat and drain the peas, reserving the cooking liquid.

In a blender, combine the peas and about 1/4 cup of the cooking liquid and purée until smooth. Add 2 tablespoons of the olive oil and process until a smooth and creamy purée forms. If it is too stiff, add a little more cooking liquid. Season to taste with salt and pepper. Spoon the warm pea purée into 4 shallow bowls and keep the purée warm while you cook the shrimp. (If you have prepared

the purée ahead of time, reserve the remaining cooking liquid to add if the mixture thickens too much before serving. Reheat it gently until warm and thin as needed.)

Spread some flour in a shallow bowl. Dip the shrimp in the flour, coating evenly and tapping off the excess.

In a sauté pan, warm the remaining 2 tablespoons olive oil over medium heat. Add the garlic and sauté for a minute or two to release its fragrance; do not let it color. Add the shrimp and cook, turning once, until they turn pink, 2 to 3 minutes. Add the wine and let it bubble up. Season the shrimp with salt and pepper.

Distribute the shrimp evenly among the bowls, placing them on top of the pea purée. Garnish each portion with parsley and a drizzle of olive oil. Serve immediately.

SERVES 4

WINE: The white blends from Friuli or Alto Adige will complement this antipasto. Look for one of these unique wines: Movia Veliko Bianco, Jermann Vintage Tunina, Vie di Romans Flor di Uis, or J. Hofstätter Barthenau Vigna San Michele. If you cannot find these labels, select a Pinot Bianco from J. Hofstätter, Alois Lageder, or Colterenzio.

Scampi al pompelmo Shrimp with Grapefruit

2 grapefruits, about 1 pound each

1 to 2 small bunches watercress, tough stems removed

16 large or jumbo shrimp, 1 1/2 to 2 pounds total, peeled and deveined

Salt and freshly ground white pepper

Juice of 1 large lemon (scant 1/2 cup)

1/4 cup dry vermouth

2 tablespoons Cognac

3 tablespoons unsalted butter, cut into cubes

Chopped fresh mint or chervil for garnish

The theme of fruit and shrimp is popular with contemporary chefs practicing *la cucina creativa*. Rome-based Gianfranco Vissani pairs shrimp with a little stew of zucchini, melon, and apples, and adorns the shellfish with truffle water and oyster butter. It is a bit over the top for me, but the zucchini, apple, and melon mixture might be fun. He also makes a salad of artichokes, melon, and mint with *guanciale*- or pancetta-wrapped shrimp. But I was especially taken with this recipe that pairs sweet shrimp and tart grapefruit, an inspiration of the late Angelo Paracucchi. You can serve them on a bed of watercress, baby arugula, or even with sliced cooked artichoke hearts. Pink grapefruit segments are prettier, as their color echoes that of the shrimp, but white ones will work as well.

○ ○ ○

Working with 1 grapefruit at a time, cut a thin slice off the top and bottom to reveal the flesh. Stand the grapefruit upright and remove the peel in wide strips, cutting downward and following the contour of the fruit. Holding the grapefruit over a bowl, cut along both sides of each segment, releasing the segments from the membrane and allowing them to drop into the bowl. Using the knife tip, pry out any seeds from the segments. Squeeze the membrane over another bowl to release the juice. Repeat with the remaining grapefruit. You should have about 1/2 cup juice.

Arrange a bed of watercress on 4 salad plates or on a single large platter. Sprinkle the shrimp with salt and white pepper and set aside.

In a large sauté pan, combine the lemon juice, vermouth, and Cognac over medium-high heat and cook until reduced by half, just a couple of minutes. Add the reserved grapefruit juice to the pan and bring to a boil. Add the shrimp to the pan and cook, turning once, until they turn pink and are cooked through, 4 to 6 minutes total, depending on the size of the shrimp. Remove the pan from the heat and arrange the shrimp on top of the watercress, alternating them with the grapefruit segments.

Return the pan to high heat and cook the pan juices until they are reduced to 6 tablespoons. Whisk the butter into the pan juices a little at a time, stirring until a nice sauce consistency forms.

Spoon the sauce over the shrimp and top with the mint. Serve warm.

SERVES 4 TO 6

Variation

Add 2 artichokes hearts, cooked and sliced lengthwise, to the salad, alternating them with the grapefruit and shrimp. You can trim and cook 2 artichokes as directed for Preserved Artichokes (page 84, for short-term storage), using only the olive oil and water for cooking, and then drain, cool, slice, and use them as they are, rather than preserving them in olive oil.

WINE: You have three excellent options here. You can pour a Vermentino from Sardinia or Liguria, from Contini or Cantina Sociale Gallura; a Greco di Tufo from Campania, from Villa Raiano, Vesevo, or Villa Matilde; or a Falanghina from Campania, from Feudi di San Gregorio, Vesevo, or Villa Raiano. If serving the variation with artichokes, pour a Prosecco or Franciacorta.

Insalata di fagioli e gamberi White Bean Salad with Shrimp

For the bean salad

1½ cups dried *cannellini* or Great Northern beans

3 teaspoons salt

⅓ cup plus ½ cup extra-virgin olive oil

3 to 4 tablespoons fresh lemon juice or mild white wine vinegar

½ teaspoon freshly ground black pepper

1 cup finely chopped red onion

1 cup peeled, chopped tomatoes

2 tablespoons chopped fresh basil, mint, or flat-leaf parsley

Beans are neutral in flavor, so they provide an excellent background for more dramatic flavors. Tuscan cooks prefer white beans such as *cannellini,* while in the north, *borlotti* are the legume of choice. Umbrian cooks reach for the local lentils, and in the south, chickpeas and favas prevail. Bean salads can be served on their own, paired with other cooked and marinated vegetable salads, or topped with various cured meats cut into narrow strips. But bean salads truly shine when they are paired with seafood. The classic Tuscan white bean salad is topped with canned tuna and red onion (see variations). It can be made a bit more upscale by using cooked shellfish such as lobster, octopus, or shrimp (as is the case here) in place of the tuna.

Contemporary chefs like to serve the beans or the shellfish, or both, warm. This makes the salad a dish that needs last-minute attention, but it is more sensual and dramatic. At Ristorante San Domenico di Imola, in Emilia-Romagna, the shrimp are cooked in white wine with a crushed garlic clove. The beans are dressed with olive oil and lemon, chopped basil

and parsley, and diced tomatoes. The shrimp, along with a bit of their cooking liquid, are added to the salad while they are still warm.

○○○

To prepare the beans, pick them over, rinse well, place in a bowl with water to cover generously, and soak overnight. (If you did not remember to soak the beans, you can use the quick-soak method: Put the beans in a saucepan with ample water to cover and place over high heat. Bring to a boil, boil for 2 minutes, and remove from the heat. Cover, let stand for 1 hour, and then drain.)

Drain the beans and place in a saucepan with water to cover by 2 inches. Bring to a boil over medium high heat, reduce the heat to low, cover, and simmer gently until tender but not soft, about 40 minutes. Add 2 teaspoons of the salt after the first 10 minutes of cooking. When the beans are ready, remove from the heat, drain, and place in a bowl. You should have about 3 cups beans.

While the beans are still quite warm, add the ⅓ cup olive oil, 3 tablespoons lemon juice, the remaining 1 teaspoon salt, and the ½ teaspoon pepper. Toss well and taste and adjust the seasoning with more lemon

Extra-virgin olive oil for sautéing and drizzling

24 large or medium shrimp, peeled and deveined

1/4 cup dry white wine

Salt

Fresh lemon juice or mild white wine vinegar for drizzling (optional)

2 tablespoons chopped fresh basil, mint, or flat-leaf parsley

juice and pepper. Let the beans sit for a while until they are just warm or at room temperature; as they cool, they will absorb the flavor of the dressing. Add the remaining 1/2 cup olive oil, the onion, tomatoes, and basil. Mix well, then taste and adjust the seasoning with salt and pepper. You may want to add more lemon juice or vinegar, too. This is a basic bean salad.

To garnish the salad with the shrimp, pour enough olive oil into a sauté pan to form a light film on the bottom and heat over high heat. Add the shrimp and the wine and sauté the shrimp until they turn pink and are cooked through, 3 to 4 minutes. Remove from the heat.

To serve, arrange the warm shrimp on top of the beans (they can still be lukewarm or they can be at room temperature). Sprinkle with a little salt, drizzle with olive oil, and then drizzle with lemon juice, if desired. Top with the basil. Serve immediately.

SERVES 6

Variations: You can substitute 1 1/2 cups lentils for the white beans. Pick over and rinse, but omit the soaking. Place in a saucepan with water to cover by 3 inches and cook as directed. They will be tender in 20 to 50 minutes, depending on their age. Drain and proceed as directed.

You can use 2 live lobsters in place of the shrimp. See Lobster Salad with Pesto (page 115) for cooking, shelling, and cutting instructions. (If you are pressed for time, buy 2 cooked lobsters at your fish market.)

You can use 2 cans (6 ounces each) olive oil–packed tuna, drained and broken into good-sized flakes, in place of the shrimp. Top with 1/4 cup chopped or shaved red onion.

The late Ligurian chef Angelo Paracucchi served cooked scampi atop a bed of white bean purée. To purée the beans, cook as directed but do not drain, and then purée the beans with their cooking liquid in a food processor.

WINE: This antipasto mates well with a number of Italian whites. Try Greco di Tufo from Campania, from producers such as Feudi di San Gregorio, Vesevo, or Villa Raiano. Or, pour a Piedmontese Roero Arneis from Ceretto, Giacosa, or Malvira. A Falerio from the Marche is yet another complementary choice, with Pilastri, San Giovanni, and Velenosi among the best producers.

Involtini di gamberi rossi in umido di ceci
Prosciutto-Wrapped Shrimp with Warm Chickpea Salad

1 cup dried chickpeas

4 tablespoons extra-virgin olive oil, plus oil for drizzling

Salt

12 jumbo shrimp, peeled and deveined

6 large slices prosciutto, cut in half lengthwise

2 fresh rosemary sprigs

1 large clove garlic, crushed

2 tomatoes, peeled and diced (fresh or canned)

Freshly ground black pepper

2 tablespoons chopped fresh flat-leaf parsley

At Ristorante San Domenico di Imola, chef Valentino Marcattilii includes this glamorous variation on the classic bean and seafood salad on his menu. It is served warm and makes a memorable opener to a meal. Chickpeas tend to be starchier and a bit heavier than white beans. Serving them warm lightens their texture.

∘∘∘

To prepare the chickpeas, pick them over, rinse well, place in a bowl with water to cover generously, and soak overnight. (If you did not remember to soak the chickpeas, you can use the quick-soak method: Put the chickpeas in a saucepan with ample water to cover and place over high heat. Bring to a boil, boil for 2 minutes, and remove from the heat. Cover, let stand for 1 hour, and then drain.)

Drain the chickpeas. In a saucepan, combine the chickpeas with water to cover by 2 inches. Add 1 tablespoon of the olive oil, bring to a boil over medium-high heat, reduce the heat to low, cover, and simmer gently until tender but not soft, 40 to 50 minutes. Add 2 teaspoons salt after the first 10 minutes of cooking. When the chickpeas are ready, remove from the heat and set aside; keep warm.

Wrap each shrimp in a strip of prosciutto and secure in place with a toothpick. In a large sauté pan, warm the remaining 3 tablespoons olive oil over medium heat. Add the rosemary and garlic and sauté for a minute or two to flavor the oil. Add the shrimp and sauté, turning once, until the prosciutto is lightly colored on both sides and the shrimp are pink, 6 to 8 minutes total. Transfer the shrimp to a platter, discard the toothpicks, and keep warm.

Return the sauté pan to low heat and add the tomatoes and the chickpeas and just enough of their cooking liquid to moisten slightly. Season with salt and pepper and simmer for 5 minutes to blend the flavors. Remove and discard the garlic and rosemary, then taste and adjust the seasoning with salt and pepper.

Place a spoonful of chickpeas on each plate, or spoon them all onto a platter. Top with the shrimp and garnish with the parsley. Drizzle olive oil over the top. Serve warm.

SERVES 4

NOTE: *If you are pressed for time, you can use 2 cups drained canned chickpeas. Rinse them well and add to the sauté pan with the tomatoes, a little stock or water in place of the cooking liquid, and 1 tablespoon extra-virgin olive oil. Proceed as directed.*

WINE: Tre Monti's Albana di Romagna Secco is a wonderful wine with this dish. Albana is the local white grape of Emilia-Romagna, and though the wine is hard to find, it is worth the effort. If you cannot track it down, drink a Campanian Fiano di Avellino or Falanghina, bottled by De Conciliis, Vesevo, or Villa Raiano.

Cipollata di tonno Tuna in a Sweet-and-Sour Onion Marinade

1/4 cup extra-virgin olive oil,
plus oil for frying

4 large white onions, sliced 1/4 inch
thick

1/2 cup white wine vinegar

1/4 cup raisins, plumped in hot water
and drained (optional)

1/4 cup pine nuts, toasted (optional)

Salt and freshly ground black pepper

1 1/2 pounds firm tuna fillets

For *cipollata di tonno,* fresh tuna is smothered in an onion (*cipolla*) marinade. Sometimes this marination technique is called *à scupece* (related to the Spanish *escabeche*), and in Venice it is called *in saor,* "with flavor." Pine nuts and raisins are optional additions and, of course, will make the onions sweeter. The meaty character of tuna is a nice foil for the sweet onions. You can use a milder fish fillet such as sole, or one that is stronger, say mackerel. Be sure to let the fish marinate for at least 6 hours, and preferably longer.

o o o

In a large sauté pan, heat the 1/4 cup olive oil over medium heat. Add the onions and cook, stirring occasionally, until tender and lightly golden, about 20 minutes. Add the vinegar and the raisins and pine nuts, if using, and cook for a few minutes longer to blend the flavors. Season with 1 teaspoon salt and 1/2 teaspoon pepper and remove from the heat. Transfer to a bowl.

Pat the tuna fillets dry and season with salt and pepper. Rinse the sauté pan, wipe dry, place over medium-high heat, and add just enough olive oil to film the bottom. When hot, add the fish in batches and fry, turning once, until golden on both sides and cooked through, 5 to

6 minutes for each batch. Using a slotted spatula, carefully transfer the cooked fish to a platter.

When all the fish are cooked, top them with the warm onion mixture. Cover and marinate for up to 2 hours at cool room temperature or for up to 24 hours in the refrigerator.

Remove the tuna from the refrigerator and bring to room temperature before serving.

SERVES 6 TO 10

NOTE: *On his cooking show, chef Gianfranco Vissani has been playing the contemporary deconstruction game with traditional recipes. In his takeoff on this classic, he uses fillets of sole and rolls each fillet around a spoonful of potato purée. Then he dips the rolls in brioche crumbs, fries them, and places them on a sauce of onions and shallots simmered in beer. Finally, he soaks slices of Tropea onion in milk, deep-fries them, and scatters the crunchy onion rings over the fish rolls.*

WINE: *Rosato* from Sardinia or Abruzzo would be ideal but difficult to find. A good alternative—and easier to locate—is a *rosato* (made from the Lagrein grape) from the Alto Adige. A Fiano di Avellino from Campania is another great choice. Look for such producers as Feudi di San Gregorio, Villa Matilde, De Conciliis, Villa Raiano, and Vesevo.

Capesante alla fonduta di cipollotti novelli e tartufi neri
Scallops with Spring Onion Purée and Black Truffles

6 tablespoons extra-virgin olive oil

10 spring onions, white part only, chopped

1 ounce black truffle, chopped; 2 to 3 tablespoons black truffle paste (see note, page 41); or black truffle oil to taste

18 sea scallops, foot muscle removed

Fleur de sel

Minced fresh chives for garnish

This sensual dish of warm scallops on a bed of warm puréed spring onions enhanced with black truffles is a special-occasion antipasto. It is the creation of chef Ezio Santin, who serves it at Antica Osteria del Ponte in Cassinetta di Lugagnano, not far from Milan. The harmonious blend of tender scallops with golden, crunchy tops, flavorful *fleur de sel,* and rich, sweet onion purée perfumed with truffle makes this an incredibly voluptuous dish. In place of fresh truffles, you may add some truffle paste to the onion purée, or a few judicious drops of truffle oil. But even without truffles, this dish is delicious. If the scallops are very large, serve only two per person, as they are quite rich.

○ ○ ○

In a large sauté pan, heat 3 tablespoons of the olive oil over low heat. Add the onions and sauté for 8 minutes. Add a few tablespoons water and continue to cook, stirring occasionally, until the onions are very soft, 8 to 10 minutes longer. Remove from the heat, transfer to a blender, and purée until smooth. You should have about 2 cups purée. Stir the truffle into the purée and keep warm.

In a large nonstick sauté pan, heat the remaining 3 tablespoons olive oil over high heat. Add the scallops and sauté, turning once, until golden on the outside and just opaque at the center, 4 to 6 minutes total.

Divide the onion purée evenly among warmed salad plates. Top with the scallops, again dividing evenly, and sprinkle with the *fleur de sel* and chives. Serve warm.

SERVES 6 TO 8

Variations:

If you cannot find spring onions (small, white bulbs on green stems), you can use 4 bunches green onions (scallions), white part only, and 1 yellow onion in their place.

In place of the truffle, trim the stem ends, wipe clean, and slice ¼ pound fresh porcini or chanterelle mushrooms, then sauté the mushrooms in olive oil until tender. Serve them with the scallops atop the onion purée.

WINE: This antipasto combines strong flavors. You need a wine that will both stand up to them and complement them. For a wine with great natural acidity and rich flavor, look no further than Verdicchio dei Castelli di Jesi. In particular, try the single vineyard bottling from Sartarelli called Tralivio. The fruit is picked late in the season, so its flavors are concentrated, giving the wine richness, ripeness, and depth, while its freshness is maintained.

Insalata di capesante e funghi porcini
Warm Salad of Scallops and Porcini

¼ pound fresh porcini mushrooms

1 large tomato, peeled, seeded, and diced (fresh or canned)

6 tablespoons extra-virgin olive oil

Salt and freshly ground black pepper

1 tablespoon aged balsamic vinegar

¼ pound small, slender green beans, trimmed

12 sea scallops, foot muscle removed

¼ pound arugula, tough stems removed

2 tablespoons chopped fresh flat-leaf parsley

Trattoria dall'Amelia in Venice serves sautéed porcini and scallops atop a bed of arugula. The combination of mushrooms and seafood is particularly rich, so the greens provide contrast and relief. In place of fresh porcini, you can use chanterelle, matsutake, hen-of-the-woods, or cremini mushrooms. The original recipe calls for roasting the mushrooms and tomato, but sautéing works equally well. I give both methods here, so you can choose. If you find arugula too peppery for your taste, use a milder lettuce.

○○○

Trim the stem ends on the mushrooms and then wipe the mushrooms clean with damp paper towels.

To roast the mushrooms and tomato, preheat the oven to 400°F. Combine the mushrooms and tomato in a baking dish. Drizzle with 2 tablespoons of the olive oil, sprinkle with salt and pepper, and mix well. Roast until the mushrooms are tender, about 10 minutes. Remove from the oven, sprinkle with the vinegar, stir well, and keep warm.

Alternatively, to cook the mushrooms and tomato on the stove top, heat 2 tablespoons of the olive oil in a sauté pan over medium heat. Add the mushrooms and sauté for about 5 minutes. Add the tomato and cook until the mushrooms and tomato are tender, 2 to 3 minutes longer.

Season with salt and pepper and remove from the heat. Sprinkle with the vinegar, stir well, and keep warm.

Meanwhile, bring a saucepan filled with salted water to a boil over high heat. Add the green beans, and boil until tender-crisp, 2 to 3 minutes. Drain and refresh in a bowl filled with ice water. When cold, drain again, pat dry, and set aside.

In a large, nonstick sauté pan, heat 3 tablespoons of the olive oil over medium-high heat. Add the scallops and sauté, turning once, until they take on some color and are just opaque at the center, 4 to 6 minutes total. Remove from the heat.

In a bowl, combine the green beans, arugula, the remaining 1 tablespoon olive oil, and a little salt and toss to coat evenly. Distribute the beans and arugula among 4 salad plates. Top with the mushrooms and then the scallops. Sprinkle with the parsley and serve warm.

SERVES 4

WINE: Red or white? You could go with a light, zippy red, such as a Lagrein from Alto Adige, to play off the rich and aromatic porcini. J. Hofstätter, Elena Walch, and Terlano all make good ones. For a white wine, turn to Friuli for a Ribolla, Tocai Friulano, or Pinot Bianco, from Movia, Scarbolo, Schioppetto, Antico Broilo, or La Castellada.

Sarde a beccaficcu Sicilian Stuffed Sardines

2 1/2 pounds fresh sardines (about 24)

7 tablespoons extra-virgin olive oil, plus oil for preparing dish

1 cup fine dried bread crumbs

2 cloves garlic, finely minced

1/3 cup pine nuts, toasted and chopped

1/3 cup currants, plumped in hot water, drained, and chopped

2 to 3 tablespoons capers, rinsed

3 tablespoons chopped fresh flat-leaf parsley

1/4 cup grated pecorino cheese (optional)

Salt and freshly ground pepper

Bay leaves (optional)

2 to 3 tablespoons fresh lemon juice

1/4 cup fresh orange juice (optional)

The *beccafico,* a tiny bird that becomes fat from gorging on figs (*fichi*), is the inspiration for the name of this dish. When the sardines are stuffed and rolled, they are thought to resemble the fruit-loving birds. Some recipes recommend putting bay leaves between the rolled fish; others mix grated cheese into the filling. In Catania, cooks add diced *caciocavallo* cheese to the filling, and the stuffed sardines are dipped in flour and fried instead of baked. Other Sicilian cooks dip the fish in flour, then beaten egg, and finally in fine dried bread crumbs and fry them. The sardines are a versatile addition to an antipasto assortment.

o o o

To clean each sardine, cut off the head and fins and then remove any scales. Split the fish open along the belly and remove the viscera. Run your index finger inside the fish the length of the backbone so that the fish opens flat like a book. Lift up and remove the backbone, breaking it off at the tail. Repeat with the remaining fish. Rinse all the fish well, pat dry, and set aside.

To make the filling, in a small sauté pan, heat 3 tablespoons of the olive oil over medium-high heat. Add the bread crumbs and cook, stirring constantly, until well moistened, about 3 minutes. Add the garlic and cook, stirring, for 2 minutes longer. Remove from the heat and add the pine nuts, currants, capers, parsley, and the cheese, if using. Mix well and season to taste with salt and pepper.

Select a baking dish just large enough to accommodate the sardines once they are rolled, and lightly oil the dish. Open a sardine flat, skin side down, and place a heaping teaspoonful of the filling near the top. Starting at the head end, bring it over the filling and roll the fish toward the tail. Place the rolled fish, tail up, in the prepared baking dish. Repeat with the remaining sardines and filling, packing them tightly so they don't unroll. Slip bay leaves between the fish rolls, if you like. (You can assemble the sardine rolls up to this point and refrigerate for up to 4 hours before continuing.)

Preheat the oven to 400°F.

In a small bowl, whisk together the remaining 4 tablespoons olive oil, the lemon juice, and the orange juice, if using. Pour over the sardines. Bake until the fish are firm, about 10 minutes. Serve hot, warm, or at room temperature.

SERVES 10 TO 12

WINE: Pair this antipasto with a white wine from southern Italy, such as a Vermentino from Sardinia or a Fiano di Avellino from Campania, or with a Falerio from the Marche.

Calamari ripieni Stuffed Squid

10 tablespoons extra-virgin olive oil

1 1/2 cups chopped yellow onion

4 cloves garlic, minced

12 medium or 16 small squid, cleaned, bodies left whole, and tentacles chopped

1 to 1 1/2 cups fresh bread crumbs

1/4 cup grated pecorino cheese (optional)

2 teaspoons grated lemon zest (optional)

5 tablespoons fresh lemon juice

6 tablespoons chopped fresh flat-leaf parsley

Salt and freshly ground black pepper

3 tablespoons capers, rinsed

Stuffed squid are popular in southern Italy. Bread crumbs, along with garlic and onion, are the base of the classic filling. In Sardinia and Puglia, grated cheese is often added. In Sicily, some cooks mix in a little chopped anchovy, and in Naples, a pinch of dried oregano, a few chopped olives, and even some shrimp are sometimes part of the mix. To keep squid tender, you must either cook them briefly or braise them for a long time. There is no middle ground. Here, they are stuffed, quickly grilled or broiled, and dressed with olive oil, lemon juice, and capers. If you do not have a grill, you can braise the stuffed squid in a sauce of stock and wine or you can bake them (see variations).

○ ○ ○

In a sauté pan, heat 3 tablespoons of the olive oil over medium heat. Add the onion and sauté until tender, about 10 minutes. Add the garlic, the chopped squid tentacles, and 1 cup of the bread crumbs if the squid are very small, or more crumbs if the squid are larger or if the mixture seems too wet. Continue to sauté for 2 minutes, stirring often. Remove from the heat. Add the cheese and lemon zest, if using, 1 tablespoon of the lemon juice, and the parsley. Mix well and season to taste with salt and pepper. Let cool completely.

Fill the squid bodies with the stuffing, and secure the ends closed with a toothpick.

In a small bowl, whisk together 5 tablespoons of the olive oil, the remaining 4 tablespoons lemon juice, and the capers. Season to taste with salt and pepper. Set aside to use for dressing the cooked squid.

Prepare a medium-hot fire in a charcoal grill, preheat a stove-top ridged grill pan over high heat, or preheat a broiler. Thread the squid onto long metal skewers, sliding 2 squid onto each skewer if using small squid and 1 squid onto each skewer if using larger ones. Brush the squid with the remaining 2 tablespoons olive oil, and sprinkle with salt and pepper.

Place the skewered squid on the grill rack, on the grill pan, or on a broiler pan and slip under the broiler. Grill or broil, turning once, until the squid are opaque and the filling is warm, about 3 minutes on each side.

When the squid are ready, transfer them to a platter or individual plates, sliding them free of the skewers. Remove the toothpicks and spoon the caper dressing over the top. Serve hot or warm.

SERVES 6 TO 8

Variations:

To braise the stuffed squid, stuff the squid as directed and omit the caper dressing and the remaining 2 tablespoons olive oil. In a heavy pot, heat 3 tablespoons olive oil over medium heat. Add 1 yellow onion, chopped, and 1 carrot, peeled and chopped, and cook, stirring, until very soft, about 15 minutes. Add 1 bay leaf, 1 cup fish stock, and 1 cup dry white wine and bring to a simmer. Add the squid, reduce the heat to low, cover, and simmer until the squid are tender, 45 to 60 minutes. Season to taste with salt and pepper.

To bake the stuffed squid, preheat the oven to 350°F. Stuff the squid as directed and arrange in a baking dish. In a small bowl, stir together the remaining 2 tablespoons olive oil and 1 cup dry white wine. Lightly brush the squid with some of the wine mixture. Bake the squid, basting often with the wine mixture, until tender, about 45 minutes. Serve with the caper dressing.

For an alternative stuffing, sauté 1 small yellow onion, chopped, in 2 tablespoons olive oil over medium heat until tender, about 10 minutes. Add the chopped squid tentacles and sauté for 2 minutes. Remove from the heat and add 1 1/2 cups fresh bread crumbs; 1/2 cup raisins, plumped in hot water and drained; 1/2 cup pine nuts, toasted; and 1 egg, lightly beaten. Season with salt and pepper.

WINE: Look for a Sicilian white blend from Spadafora, Mirabile, or Donnafugata. If you cannot find these wines, stay with a white from southern Italy, such as a Falanghina from Campania.

Baccalà mantecato Whipped Salt Cod Spread

1 pound boneless salt cod

Polenta crostini or grilled or toasted bread for serving

Whole milk for cooking (optional), plus warmed milk, if needed

1/3 cup extra-virgin olive oil, or as needed

1 or 2 cloves garlic, finely minced

2 tablespoons finely chopped fresh flat-leaf parsley

Salt and freshly ground black pepper

Baccalà mantecato is a signature dish of the Venetian kitchen and is served in almost all the local *bacari* (wine bars). The easiest way to serve this purée of salt cod is slightly warm, in a bowl or crock, surrounded by pieces of toasted or grilled bread or spread on polenta crostini. A more spectacular way of serving, it is spooned on top of a bed of soft, warm polenta. Contemporary chefs sometimes top it with a bit of caviar.

o o o

In a bowl or other vessel, combine the salt cod with water to cover and refrigerate for 1 to 2 days, changing the water at least 3 times. The soaking time will depend on the saltiness of the cod and the thickness of the pieces; thicker pieces will take longer than thinner pieces.

Before you cook and purée the cod, you need to decide whether you will be serving it with polenta crostini or with toasted or grilled bread. If you are serving it with the polenta crostini, make, chill, and cut the polenta into the shape of choice as directed for Fried Polenta with Cheese Spread (page 72). If you want to grill, broil, or bake the cutouts, brush them with olive oil and ready a hot charcoal fire in the grill, preheat the broiler, or preheat the oven to 400°F. If you want to fry the polenta cutouts, leave them plain. If you are serving the salt cod with grilled or toasted bread, ready a charcoal fire, preheat the broiler, or ready a toaster oven.

Drain the salt cod and place in a saucepan. Add water or equal parts water and milk to cover and bring slowly to a gentle simmer. Cook over low heat until the fish is tender, 10 to 20 minutes. Drain the salt cod and let cool slightly, then break it up into 2-inch pieces, removing any errant bones, traces of skin, or discolored or tough parts.

Flake the warm fish with your fingers into a food processor or into the bowl of a stand mixer fitted with the paddle attachment. Process or mix to break up the pieces into fine shreds. Gradually beat in 1/3 cup olive oil or as needed to yield a smooth purée. Taste the fish. It is unlikely that it will be too salty, but if it is, whip in some warm milk. Transfer the fish to a warmed bowl and fold in the garlic and parsley. Season with pepper and don't be surprised if you need to add a bit of salt for balance. Keep warm.

Quickly finish the polenta crostini now, grilling or broiling them, turning once, until golden and crisp; arranging on an oiled rimmed baking sheet and baking until hot and golden, or frying until golden and crisp. Or, grill or toast bread slices.

Serve the salt cod warm with the polenta crostini or bread.

SERVES 4 TO 6

WINE: Vernaccia di Oristano from Sardinia is an obscure wine that tastes like a dry amontillado sherry. It is nutty and complex and pairs well with *pesce crudo, baccalà,* and other salty treats. The only one currently imported to the United States is made by Contini, and if you search for it, you will be well rewarded. If you cannot find it, open a Verdicchio dei Castelli di Jesi from the Marche, a Fiano di Avellino from Campania, or a Vermentino, Pigato, or Bianchetta from Liguria.

Cozze al forno Baked Mussels

For the toasted bread crumbs (optional)

2 cups cubed coarse country bread (crusts removed)

3 tablespoons extra-virgin olive oil

1/2 teaspoon salt

Freshly ground black pepper

24 to 36 mussels, well scrubbed and debearded

1/2 cup dry white wine or water

2 tablespoons extra-virgin olive oil, plus oil for drizzling

2 cloves garlic, finely minced

2 tablespoons chopped fresh basil

2 tomatoes, peeled, seeded, and chopped

Freshly ground black pepper

Lemon wedges for serving

Here is a perfect small plate to accompany a glass of white or sparkling wine. What makes the dish special is texture: the crunchiness of the toasted bread crumbs atop the tender mussels. This is a house specialty of the Associazione Amici Degli Anziani in Vasto, a seacoast town in Abruzzo. If you don't have time to make your own toasted bread crumbs, use commercial dried bread crumbs. And if you cannot find good fresh mussels, clams can be used in their place.

∘∘∘

If you have time, make the toasted bread crumbs: Preheat the oven to 350°F. Pulse the bread cubes in a food processor until fine crumbs form. Transfer the crumbs to a bowl, add the olive oil, salt, and a few grinds of pepper, and toss to coat evenly. Spread the crumbs on a rimmed baking sheet, place in the oven, and toast, stirring occasionally, until the crumbs are lightly golden, about 20 minutes. Remove from the oven, pour into a shallow bowl, and let cool. Measure out 1/2 cup of the crumbs to use for the mussels. Reserve the remaining crumbs for another use. (They will keep in an airtight container at room temperature for up to 4 days; stir into pasta or sprinkle on cooked vegetables such as cauliflower or broccoli.)

Raise the oven temperature to 450°F, or preheat the broiler. Oil a gratin dish that will accommodate the shelled mussels in a single layer; make sure the dish is flameproof if you are using the broiler.

In a large, deep sauté pan, combine the mussels and wine, cover, and place over high heat. Cook just until the mussels crack open, about 3 minutes. Do not overcook. Remove the pan from the heat, and then remove the mussels from the pan, discarding any that failed to open.

Remove the mussels from their shells, allowing any of their liquid to drain back into the pan, and discard the shells and any beards that remain. Arrange the mussels in a single layer in the prepared gratin dish. Pour the liquid in the sauté pan through a cheesecloth-lined sieve placed over a bowl and set aside.

In a medium-sized sauté pan, heat the 2 tablespoons olive oil over low heat. Add the garlic and basil, stir for a minute or two to release their flavors, and then add the tomatoes. Cook, stirring occasionally, for 10 minutes, adding mussel liquid as needed to keep the mixture moist and spoonable.

Remove from the heat and pour the tomato mixture evenly over the mussels. Top evenly with the 1/2 cup bread crumbs and a few grinds of pepper, and drizzle with extra-virgin olive oil. Place in the oven and bake until the crumbs are golden, about 10 minutes. Or, slip under the broiler about 4 inches from the heat source and broil until the crumbs are golden, 3 to 4 minutes.

Remove the dish from the oven and serve immediately with the lemon wedges.

SERVES 4

Variations:

For a more dramatic presentation, save the bottom shell of each mussel, return a mussel to each shell, and top with the tomato mixture and then the crumbs. You can also stir 3 tablespoons grated Parmesan cheese into the bread crumbs before sprinkling them on top.

WINE: Prosecco pairs beautifully with this antipasto. If you prefer a white wine, choose one that is neither too big nor too oaky, such as a Falanghina, Gavi di Gavi, or Vermentino.

Tartine di patate con pesce affumicato e caviale
Potato Cakes with Smoked Fish and Caviar

Olive oil for preparing molds

2 large russet potatoes, about 1½ pounds total weight, peeled and diced

Salt

2 egg yolks

2 tablespoons unsalted butter, at room temperature

¼ teaspoon freshly grated nutmeg

Freshly ground black pepper

1 cup plain full-fat yogurt

2 tablespoons heavy cream

6 tablespoons caviar

3 tablespoons chopped fresh dill or chives

½ pound smoked salmon or smoked trout fillets, cut into strips

When Ermenegildo Muzzolini was the chef at Rome's La Pergola restaurant, he served this dish. The potato cakes are an ideal neutral base for the salty fish and succulent roe. I love the contrast of the warm potato cake and the cool sauce. If the caviar seems too pricey, the dish is still delicious without it.

∘∘∘

Oil eight ¾-cup custard cups or ramekins.

In a saucepan, combine the potatoes with water to cover, add a little salt, and bring to a boil over high heat. Cook until tender, about 15 minutes. Drain and pass through a ricer held over a bowl. Add the egg yolks, butter, nutmeg, 2 teaspoons salt, and a few grinds of pepper and mix well. Let rest for 10 minutes.

Preheat the oven to 450°F.

Divide the potato mixture evenly among the prepared molds, and press firmly into the molds. The potato mixture should be about 1 inch high. Arrange the molds on a rimmed baking sheet.

In a bowl, stir together the yogurt, cream, 2 tablespoons of the caviar, and 1 tablespoon of the dill. Taste and adjust the seasoning with salt, remembering that you will be adding smoked fish and more caviar, both of which are salty. Set aside.

Place the molds in the oven and bake just until the potato layer has set up, 8 to 10 minutes. Remove from the oven. To unmold each potato cake, run a thin knife blade around the inside of the mold to loosen the sides, invert a plate on top, invert the mold and plate together, and lift off the mold.

Top each potato cake with an equal amount of the smoked fish and then the caviar sauce. Garnish with the remaining 4 tablespoons caviar and 2 tablespoons dill, dividing them evenly. Serve warm.

SERVES 8

WINE: *Spumante* Ca' del Bosco, Prosecco, or Franciacorta would be spectacular with this antipasto. If you prefer a still wine, try an aromatic white from Alto Adige, such as the J. Hofstätter Barthenau Vigna San Michele; a Gewürztraminer from the same vintner; or a white from Colterenzio or Elena Walch. Other great producers working with local grapes in the Italian Alps include Cantina Valle Isarco, St. Michael-Eppan, and Alois Lageder.

Insalata di polpo e patate Octopus and Potato Salad

1 octopus, about 2 pounds, cleaned

3 tablespoons olive oil

1 pound small new potatoes

Salt

$1/2$ cup extra-virgin olive oil, or as needed

$1/4$ cup fresh lemon juice

$1/2$ red onion, minced

2 cloves garlic, minced

2 tablespoons grated lemon zest (optional)

Freshly ground black pepper

Red pepper flakes (optional)

Black olives for garnish (optional)

Chopped fresh flat-leaf parsley for garnish

Not every fish market stocks octopus, but when you can find it, it is likely to have been frozen. The smaller ones usually weigh about two pounds, or sometimes you can get a portion of a larger one. If you are lucky, it will have been blanched (if it has, it will be purple) and cleaned. If not, the job is yours. Cut off the top of the head, turn it inside out, and discard the organs. Cut away the eyes, and then press on the body to expel the beak.

Cooking techniques vary. Some cooks simmer octopus in water with a carrot, a celery stalk, an onion, and a sprig of parsley and let it cool in the cooking liquid. Some abide by the folklore of placing a cork in the water, believing it will help tenderize the flesh. I find cooking in water to be a gamble. The octopus can seize up and stay tough. I prefer the technique told to me by Paola de Mauro, a famous Roman home cook and winery owner. She says use no water. Instead, she lets the octopus stew in its own juices.

If you cannot find an octopus, you can use squid in its place (see variation). A simple citrus vinaigrette is ideal for this salad. Lemon juice with a bit of lemon zest is the liveliest, but you could add a little orange juice, if you like. This recipe comes from Trattoria Nuovo Piccolo Mondo in San Remo, on the Ligurian coast.

o o o

Preheat the oven to 300°F.

Place the cleaned octopus in a saucepan pan with no liquid except for the olive oil. Place over low heat, cover, and cook until the octopus has released its liquid, about 20 minutes. Transfer the octopus and released liquid to a baking pan, cover with aluminum foil, and bake until the octopus is soft (or relatively soft; it is rather chewy by nature), 1 to $1 1/2$ hours. Remove from the oven and let cool for a bit. Peel away the purple skin and most of the suckers will come away too. Cut into bite-sized pieces. You should have $1/2$ to $3/4$ pound. Place in a serving bowl.

While the octopus is cooking, in a saucepan, combine the potatoes with salted water to cover and bring to a boil. Cook until the potatoes are tender but not soft, 10 to 15 minutes. Drain and, when cool enough to handle, cut into small pieces and add to the bowl holding the octopus.

Add the 1/2 cup extra virgin olive oil, the lemon juice, onion, garlic, lemon zest (if using), and salt and black pepper to taste and toss and stir to coat evenly. Season with red pepper flakes, if you like, and then taste and adjust the flavors with more olive oil, salt, and black pepper.

Garnish with the olives, if desired, and the parsley. Serve warm or at room temperature.

SERVES 6

Variation: To use squid in place of the octopus, clean 1 1/2 pounds squid, cut the bodies into rings 1 inch wide, and leave the tentacles whole if small or halve them if large. Bring a saucepan filled with water to a boil over high heat. Lightly salt the water, add the squid, reduce the heat to medium, and simmer until the squid are opaque, 1 1/2 to 2 minutes. Drain well, place in a serving bowl, and proceed as directed.

WINE: Drink a Vermentino from Sardinia, a Verdicchio or Trebbiano from the Marche, a Falanghina from Campania, or a white blend from Sicily.

Carne e pollame
Meat and Poultry

Antipasto is the tempting start to a meal, an appetite arouser, therefore substantial dishes based on meat and poultry are not in abundance, as they are too filling. Veal and beef carpaccio, *carne cruda* (chopped raw veal or beef served as tartare), plus all manner of *salumi* (cured meats) are addressed in Shop-and-Serve Antipasti. In this chapter, you will find two pâtés and a few cooked meat and poultry dishes served at room temperature or warm, plus some delightful meat-stuffed olives. If you were planning an antipasto buffet, the pâtés, rabbit, and chicken would be fine choices for the assortment. For a simple antipasto, try the chicken liver crostini or the fried olives.

Tonno di gallina sott'olio
Chicken Treated as Tuna, Preserved in Oil

For cooking the chicken

1 free-range chicken, 3 to 4 pounds

1 celery stalk

1 carrot

1 small yellow onion stuck with
5 whole cloves

4 quarts water

3 cloves garlic, sliced

2 or 3 bay leaves

Freshly ground black pepper

Extra-virgin olive oil to cover

4 quail eggs or small chicken eggs,
hard-boiled, peeled, and cut in half

Assorted lettuces

10 to 12 radishes, trimmed and
thinly sliced

1 celery root, peeled, thinly sliced
or shredded, and tossed with fresh
lemon juice to prevent discoloration,
or 2 bulbs fennel, trimmed, cored,
and thinly sliced lengthwise

In the contemporary Italian kitchen, chefs cover cooked veal, pork, or poultry with extra-virgin olive oil and marinate it in the refrigerator for a few days, treating it as if it were oil-preserved tuna. The olive oil marinade is thought to tenderize the flesh. A dish prepared in this manner is typically called *tonno di vitello,* "veal as tuna," or *tonno di gallina,* "chicken as tuna," as this one is. This recipe comes from the Taverna di Campagna dal 1997, in the Piedmontese town of Camagna, near Alessandria, and the key to its success is a flavorful chicken and high-quality olive oil. The chef garnishes the salad with black truffle, but it isn't needed. The platter is wonderfully festive—and completely satisfying—without it.

○○○

To cook the chicken, rinse it well inside and out and place in a pot. Add the celery, carrot, onion, and water and bring to a gentle boil over medium-high heat, skimming off any foam that forms on the surface. Reduce the heat to low, cover, and simmer very gently until the chicken is just tender when tested with a knife tip, 1 1/4 to 1 1/2 hours. Remove from the heat and let the chicken cool in the broth. Remove the cooled chicken to a cutting board. Strain the broth and reserve for another use; it will taste subtly of clove.

Discard the skin from the chicken, then remove all of the meat from the bones and discard the bones. Place the meat in a colander and let drain for 30 minutes. Then cut or tear the meat into large bite-sized pieces and place in a bowl.

Add the garlic, bay leaves, and a few grinds of pepper to the bowl and toss to mix well. Transfer the chicken mixture to a 2-quart nonreactive container, press down, and pour in olive oil to immerse fully. Cover and store in the refrigerator for 2 to 3 days before serving.

3 ounces sheep's milk cheese such
as *pecorino fresco, pecorino sardo,*
or *cacioricotta,* crumbled

Salt

Aged balsamic vinegar

1 black truffle, chopped (optional)

To serve, remove from the refrigerator and let come to room temperature so that the olive oil, which will have solidified, will become liquid again. (Or, you can warm it slightly in a microwave oven.) Remove the chicken from the container, shaking any excess oil back into the container, and place the chicken in the center of a platter. Surround the chicken with the eggs, lettuces, radishes, and celery root. Top the chicken with the crumbled cheese.

Add a sprinkle of salt and some drops of aged balsamic vinegar to the oil remaining in the container, whisk well, and pour over the chicken and the vegetables. Sprinkle with the truffle, if using. Serve immediately.

SERVES 8 TO 10

Variation:

Preserved Artichokes (page 84) and/or Marinated Mushrooms (page 93) would also be good additions to the platter as a balance to the richness of the chicken.

WINE: To cut the richness of the chicken, open a bottle of Barbera from the Piedmont or a Rosso Piceno from the Marche.

Olive alla marchigiana Meat-Stuffed Fried Olives

For the filling

2 tablespoons olive oil

1 small yellow onion, chopped

¼ pound ground lean beef or veal

¼ pound ground lean pork

¼ pound ground chicken or turkey, or additional beef or veal

½ cup meat or chicken stock

2 eggs

¾ cup grated Parmesan cheese

¼ teaspoon freshly grated nutmeg or pinch of ground cinnamon

80 large green olives, pitted

1 cup all-purpose flour

2 eggs

1 cup fine dried bread crumbs

Olive oil for deep-frying

When I have traveled through the Marche and Abruzzo, I have noticed that every small restaurant—even tiny pizzerias—offers this antipasto. Cooks use the huge green olives from Ascoli Piceno, a border town between the two regions. We can find these giants at the market, but they are not always pitted, and some pitted green olives are too small to stuff. My solution is to buy large green olives that come prestuffed with pimientos, garlic, or almonds. The fillings are easy to remove, and the process takes less time than pitting eighty olives. Why make eighty? Watch them vanish as you serve them to your guests. Any you do not serve can be saved in the refrigerator to be fried the next day.

○ ○ ○

To make the filling, in a large sauté pan, heat 2 table-spoons of the olive oil over medium heat. Add the onion and sauté until tender, 8 to 10 minutes. Add the meats and sauté, breaking them up with a fork or wooden spoon, until they lose their rawness and start to take on color, about 10 minutes. Add the stock and cook until most of it is absorbed, about 15 minutes longer.

Remove from the heat and let cool slightly. Transfer the mixture to a food processor and pulse until evenly ground. Add the eggs, cheese, and nutmeg and pulse until a smooth paste forms. If not using immediately, cover and refrigerate for up to 1 day. Bring the mixture to room temperature when you are ready to stuff the olives, or it will be too stiff to flow through a pastry-bag tip. If it is still too stiff at room temperature, thin it by whisking in a little water or stock.

Spoon the filling into a pastry bag fitted with a small plain tip and pipe the filling into the pitted olives. (At this point, the olives can be covered and refrigerated for up to 2 days before frying.)

To fry the olives, spread the flour in a shallow bowl. Break the eggs into another shallow bowl and beat until blended. Put the bread crumbs in a third shallow bowl.

Pour the olive oil to a depth of 2 to 3 inches into a heavy saucepan and heat to 350°F on a deep-frying ther-mometer. Working in batches, dip the stuffed olives in the flour, coating them evenly, then the egg, and finally in the bread crumbs. (At this point, you can cover and refrigerate the olives for up to 1 day before frying.)

Carefully drop a few of the olives into the hot oil and fry until golden, about 4 minutes. Using a slotted spoon, transfer to paper towels to drain briefly and then serve immediately. Repeat with the remaining olives, always serving them piping hot.

MAKES ABOUT 80 OLIVES

Variation:

You can substitute ¾ pound sweet Italian sausages, casings removed, for the beef, pork, and chicken and cook as directed for the meats.

WINE: Drink a wine from the Marche. Try a crisp white to refresh the palate and provide balance against the effect of deep-frying. Verdicchio (dei Castelli di Jesi or Matelica) is an excellent wine with this dish. Falerio, aromatic and packed with flavor while finishing with bright acidity, is another great choice. If you must have red wine, pour Rosso Piceno.

Crostini di fegatini di pollo alla perugina
Chicken Liver Crostini from Perugia

2 cloves garlic

4 fresh sage leaves

Generous pinch of fennel seeds

4 tablespoons olive oil

3/4 pound chicken livers, trimmed

1 to 2 tablespoon capers, rinsed

1/2 cup dry red wine

Salt and freshly ground black pepper

1 black truffle, thinly sliced

12 slices coarse country bread, halved and toasted or grilled

Chopped fresh flat-leaf parsley for garnish

Black truffles are a signature of Umbrian cuisine. The addition of a truffle slice sets these classic Perugian chicken liver crostini apart from those served in Tuscany. Of course, you do not always have access to truffles, but you can buy a jar of truffle paste in a specialty-food store and spread a little on each crostino to achieve a similar result.

The liver purée can be prepared a few hours ahead of time and kept at room temperature, or the spread can be made the day before and warmed at serving time. Just be careful not to overcook the livers. They need to be creamy and moist for this spread to hold up well. At Ristorante Giò Arte e Vini in Perugia, the chef cooks the livers with red wine, rather than the sweeter *vin santo* or Marsala *secco* used in other versions of the recipe. Why not try it both ways?

o o o

On a cutting board, finely chop together the garlic, sage, and fennel seeds.

In a small sauté pan, heat 2 tablespoons of the olive oil over medium heat. Add the garlic mixture and sauté for 1 minute to release its fragrance. Add the livers and capers and sauté for another minute to coat the livers

with the oil and seasonings. Pour in the wine, reduce the heat to low, and simmer, uncovered, for about 10 minutes. The livers should be cooked but still pink in the center.

Using a slotted spoon, transfer the livers to a food processor and pulse briefly to form a coarse purée. Do not overprocess the livers, as you want some texture. Transfer to a bowl and stir in the pan juices. Season with salt and pepper. You should have about 1 1/4 cups purée.

In a small sauté pan, heat the remaining 2 tablespoons olive oil over low heat. Add the truffle slices and sauté briefly just to warm through.

Place a slice or two of truffle on each piece of bread. Spread the chicken liver purée on the truffled bread and sprinkle with a little chopped parsley. Serve warm or at room temperature.

MAKES 12 CROSTINI

WINE: I highly recommend sparkling wine with *fegatini* preparations. If, however, you prefer a red wine, stay away from big, oak-influenced ones. You will do best with a young, fresh, earthy red, such as a Montefalco Rosso from Caprai or Adanti, or a Morellino di Scansano from Fattoria Le Pupille.

Gâteau di fegatini chiari Baked Chicken Liver Pâté

Unsalted butter for preparing mold
(optional), plus 1 cup (½ pound)
unsalted butter, at room temperature

1 teaspoon unflavored gelatin

1 tablespoon water

1 tablespoon extra-virgin olive oil

1 pound chicken livers, trimmed

Salt

¼ cup port

¼ cup Cognac

1 bay leaf

½ cup heavy cream

Black truffle paste
(optional; see note, page 41)

Freshly ground black pepper

Melted clarified unsalted butter
for filming top of pâté

Toasted bread slices for serving

If you want to see the influence of France on modern
Italian chefs, you need to look no further than
the growing presence of foie gras and of loaves of
chicken liver pâté on antipasto menus. For example,
after his travels in France, chef Gualtiero Marchesi
created his "poor man's foie gras," for which he
sautés 1½ pounds of chicken livers in 10 ounces of
clarified butter over very low heat for 20 minutes.
He uses a slotted spoon to transfer the livers to
a terrine just large enough to hold them, and then
strains the butter, pours it over the livers, and
refrigerates the terrine overnight. Marchesi pairs
the rich result with a salad of baby spinach dressed
with a mustard vinaigrette.

Other chefs are equally entranced by the French
liver pâté. Here is a signature recipe from chef Ezio
Santin of the Antica Osteria del Ponte in Cassinetta
di Lugagnano, outside of Milan. Like most pâtés,
this one is quite rich and would be best served as
part of an antipasto assortment. A big plus is that
it can be prepared well ahead of serving time.

o o o

Line a standard loaf pan with plastic wrap, allowing it
to overhang the edges by several inches. Or, butter a
nonstick standard loaf pan.

In a small bowl or custard cup, sprinkle the gelatin over
the water and leave to soften for about 5 minutes.

In a large sauté pan, melt 2 tablespoons of the butter
with the olive oil over medium heat. Add the livers and
sauté, turning occasionally, until they are cooked but
still pink in the center, 7 to 8 minutes. Sprinkle with salt.
Using a slotted spoon, transfer the chicken livers to a
blender or food processor.

Return the pan to high heat, add the port, Cognac, and
bay leaf, and deglaze the pan, scraping up any browned
bits from the pan bottom. Add the softened gelatin, stir
well, and let it dissolve in the warm pan juices. Remove
from the heat.

cont'd

Process the livers until a fairly smooth purée forms. Remove and discard the bay leaf from the sauté pan, and add the contents of the pan to the blender. Cut the remaining 14 tablespoons butter into 1-tablespoon pieces and add them one a time to the blender, processing after each addition. Add the cream and the truffle paste to taste, if using, and process until fully combined. Season to taste with salt and pepper.

Pour the mixture into the prepared loaf pan. Film the top of the pâté with clarified butter. If you have lined the pan with plastic wrap, drape it over the top of the pâté after the butter has set. If not, cover the pan with a fresh sheet of plastic wrap after the butter has set. Place in the refrigerator for at least 8 hours or up to 3 days.

To serve, if you have not lined the pan with plastic wrap, run a knife blade around the inside of the pan to loosen the sides of the pâté. Fill a basin with hot water and dip the pan for several seconds into the water almost to the rim to loosen the pâté. Invert a serving platter over the pan, invert the pan and platter together, and then lift off the pan. Peel off the plastic wrap, if used.

Serve the pâté with the toasted bread slices.

SERVES 12

WINE: With all this richness, you will be happy with Prosecco, Franciacorta, or another *spumante* wine. If you do not feel like serving a sparkling wine, pour an earthy Barbera or a Nero d'Avola.

Lingua di manzo con salsa verde Tongue with Green Sauce

1 beef tongue, about 3 pounds, well scrubbed

2 yellow onions, whole or cut in half

1 large carrot, peeled and cut in half

3 celery stalks with leaves, cut in half

12 black peppercorns

1 bay leaf

6 coriander seeds

12 to 18 new potatoes

Salt

For the green sauce

1 cup chopped fresh flat-leaf parsley

¼ cup salt-packed capers, rinsed and chopped, plus a few for optional garnish

2 tablespoons finely chopped olive oil–packed anchovy fillets (4 or 5 fillets)

¼ cup fine dried bread crumbs

4 cloves garlic, minced

¼ cup red wine vinegar

¼ cup minced yellow onion (optional)

1 cup extra-virgin olive oil

Salt and freshly ground black pepper

Many years ago, on my first visit to Florence, I ate lunch at Trattoria Camillo and ordered this classic antipasto. The buttery tongue slices and the tart *salsa verde* were a perfect match, with the sauce balancing the natural richness of the meat. If you do not like tongue, do not skip this recipe. The pungent *salsa verde* can be served on cold boiled beef or on poached chicken or fish.

∘∘∘

Place the tongue in a deep pot and add the onions, carrot, celery, peppercorns, bay leaf, coriander seeds, and water to cover. Bring to a boil over high heat, skim off any scum from the surface, reduce the heat to medium-low, cover, and simmer until the tongue is tender when pierced with a knife tip, about 3 hours.

Remove the pot from the heat and let the tongue cool in the liquid. Remove the tongue from the pot and let cool until it can be handled. Slit the skin on the tongue and peel it away. Trim the "root end" to remove any bones or gristle. Cover the tongue and refrigerate until well chilled, at least 6 hours or up to 2 days. You can strain the cooking broth and reserve for another use, or you can discard it.

In a saucepan, combine the potatoes with water to cover, add a little salt, and bring to a boil over high heat. Reduce the heat to medium and simmer until the potatoes are cooked through but still firm. The cooking time will vary with the size of the potatoes, but very small ones will cook in about 10 minutes or so and larger ones in 15 to 20 minutes. Drain and let cool completely.

To make the green sauce, in a bowl, stir together the parsley, capers, anchovies, bread crumbs, garlic, vinegar, and the onion, if using. Whisk in the olive oil and season to taste with salt and pepper.

Slice both the tongue and the boiled potatoes crosswise. Arrange 1 or more rows of each of them together on a platter, or place the tongue slices in the center of the platter and arrange the potatoes around them. Top them with the sauce, and garnish with extra capers, if desired.

SERVES 6 TO 8

WINE: Here is yet another antipasto that is complemented by a Prosecco or other sparkling wine. Or, you can pour a Vermentino from Liguria or Sardinia (look for such Sardinian producers as Argiolas or Contini), or a Verdicchio dei Castelli di Jesi from the Marche, with Sartarelli and Bucci two excellent labels.

Vitello tonnato Veal with Tuna Sauce

3 tablespoons unsalted butter

1 tablespoon olive oil, or as needed

1 boneless leg of veal, 3 pounds, rolled and tied

Salt and freshly ground black pepper

1 large yellow onion, finely diced

3 carrots, peeled and finely diced

3 celery stalks, finely diced

Equal parts dry white wine and chicken or veal stock to cover

For the tuna sauce

1 can (6 ounces) olive oil–packed tuna, undrained

8 to 12 olive oil–packed anchovy fillets, puréed (about 2 tablespoons purée)

1/4 cup fresh lemon juice

cont'd

Veal and tuna may sound like the odd couple, but braised veal with a creamy tuna sauce is a classic Piedmontese antipasto. The veal is mild and tender and a lovely foil for the rich tuna mayonnaise. You might want to try this voluptuous sauce spooned over slices of grilled eggplant or zucchini, or on cooked chicken breast. You could even serve it on slices of seared rare tuna for a double-tuna jolt.

∘ ∘ ∘

In a large Dutch oven, melt the butter with the 1 table-spoon olive oil over medium-high heat. Season the veal with salt and pepper, add to the pot, and brown well on all sides, about 8 minutes. Remove the veal from the pot and set aside.

If the butter has burned, pour it out, wipe out the pot, return the pot to medium heat, and add 3 tablespoons olive oil. Add the onion, carrots, and celery and sauté until pale gold, about 15 minutes. Return the veal to the pot and add the wine and stock almost to cover the roast. (The amount of wine and stock you will need depends on the dimensions of your braising pot.) Gradually bring the liquid to a gentle boil, reduce the heat to low, cover, and simmer until an instant-read meat thermometer inserted into the thickest part of the veal leg registers 140°F, about 1 1/2 hours or a little longer. (If you like, you can instead braise the leg in a 350°F oven for about the same amount of time.)

Remove the veal from the pot and place on a platter. Let cool, cover, and refrigerate until well chilled, at least 8 hours or up to 2 days. Strain the cooking liquid through a fine-mesh sieve and reserve.

cont'd

Vitello tonnato Veal with Tuna Sauce   cont'd

2 tablespoons white wine vinegar

3/4 cup olive oil

Salt and freshly ground black
or white pepper

Salt-packed capers, rinsed,
for garnish

Chopped fresh flat-leaf parsley
for garnish

To make the tuna sauce, in a food processor, combine the tuna with its oil, anchovies, lemon juice, and vinegar and pulse until a smooth purée forms. Then, with the motor running, start adding the olive oil slowly, drop by drop, as if you are making a mayonnaise. When the mixture begins to thicken, you can begin adding the oil in a slow, steady dribble. When all of the oil has been incorporated, season the sauce to taste with salt and pepper. If the sauce is too thick, thin with a little of the liquid reserved from cooking the veal; what you don't use, save for making veal stock. (The sauce can be made a day in advance, covered, and refrigerated; bring to room temperature before serving.)

Place the veal on a cutting board and snip and remove the strings. Cut crosswise into slices about 1/4 inch thick. Arrange on a platter or individual plates, and mask with the tuna sauce. Sprinkle with the capers and parsley and serve.

SERVES 8 TO 12

WINE: For a white to accompany this Piedmontese specialty, pour a Roero Arneis from Malvira, Giacosa, or Vietti, or a Gavi di Gavi from Villa Sparina. Or, open a Dolcetto from such producers as Oberto, Massolino, and Ceretto.

Insalata d'anatra Duck Breast Salad

1 large orange or 2 blood oranges

2 Muscovy duck breast halves, about ½ pound each

Salt and freshly ground black pepper

Pinch of ground cinnamon or cloves (optional)

1 head butter lettuce, leaves separated and torn if large

2 small heads radicchio, leaves separated and torn if large

5 tablespoons extra-virgin olive oil

2 tablespoons balsamic vinegar or raspberry vinegar

¼ cup fresh orange juice (optional)

At Ristorante Cavallo Bianco in Aosta, chef Paolo Vai combines slices of duck breast with orange segments, lettuces, and radicchio for this colorful contemporary antipasto plate. Using blood oranges would give this composed salad an even more dramatic appearance. It requires last-minute attention, as it must be served warm, so if you are serving other antipasti, keep them easy.

∘ ∘ ∘

Preheat the oven to 350°F.

Cut a thin slice off the top and bottom of the orange to reveal the flesh. Stand the orange upright and remove the peel in wide strips, cutting downward and following the contour of the fruit. Holding the orange over a bowl, cut along both sides of each segment, releasing the segments from the membrane and allowing them to drop into the bowl. Using the knife tip, pry out any seeds from the segments. Repeat if using a second orange. Set the orange segments aside.

Using a sharp knife, score the skin of the duck breast halves in a crosshatch pattern, but do not cut into the meat. Rub the duck breasts with salt and pepper, and a pinch of cinnamon, if using. Let stand at room temperature for about 30 minutes.

Heat a large ovenproof sauté pan over medium heat. When it is hot, place the duck breasts, skin side down, in the pan. Cook until the breasts render their fat, 8 to 10 minutes. Drain off the fat from the pan and slip the pan into the oven for about 8 minutes for medium-rare. (If you like, you can finish the breasts on the stove top, reducing the heat to low and sautéing, turning once, for 8 to 10 minutes.)

Transfer the duck breasts to a cutting board. Allow them to rest for 5 minutes.

Meanwhile, in a bowl, combine the lettuce and radicchio. In a small bowl, whisk together the olive oil, vinegar, and the orange juice, if using, and then whisk in salt and pepper to taste to make a vinaigrette. Drizzle most of the vinaigrette over the lettuces and toss to coat evenly. Arrange on 4 salad plates.

cont'd

Insalata d'anatra Duck Breast Salad cont'd

Cut the warm duck breasts crosswise into thin slices. Arrange the duck slices and the orange segments on the lettuces. Drizzle with the remaining vinaigrette. Serve immediately.

SERVES 4

Variations:

Toss the warm duck breast slices with thin slices of pear or apple, slivers of fennel, and the lettuces. Dress with a vinaigrette made from extra-virgin olive oil, balsamic vinegar, and fresh orange or lemon juice.

At the restaurant Cascinale Nuovo in Isola d'Asti, in the Piedmont, chef Walter Ferretti serves the warm duck breast slices with sautéed porcini mushrooms on a bed of shredded carrots dressed with olive oil and balsamic vinegar. He tops the salad with shavings of aged *robiola* cheese.

WINE: A white or a red will work here. For a white, open a Roero Arneis from Malvira or Ceretto. For a red, consider a Lagrein from the Alto Adige from J. Hofstätter, La Vis, or Colterenzio.

Insalata di coniglio con vinaigrette al tartufo
Rabbit Salad with Truffle Vinaigrette

1 rabbit, about 2½ pounds

6 tablespoons unsalted butter

Salt

1 cup haricots verts or small, young green beans, trimmed

¼ cup extra-virgin olive oil

7 tablespoons white wine vinegar

Freshly ground black pepper

1 tablespoon truffle paste (see note, page 41)

¼ cup heavy cream

1 tomato, peeled, seeded, and finely diced (about 1 cup)

2 tablespoons chopped fresh chives

¼ pound fresh cremini or white mushrooms, stem ends trimmed, wiped clean, and thinly sliced

1 large or 2 small bunches watercress, tough stems removed, or 1 head butter lettuce, leaves separated

The chef at Ristorante Il Griso, in the town of Malgrate, near Como, serves this lovely warm composed salad made from the saddle, or loin, of the rabbit. He saves the legs and bones for stock. For home cooks, who must buy a whole rabbit, it seems foolish to use only the loin for this dish, so I bone out the hind legs and use them, too. If the liver is included with the rabbit, sauté it and eat it yourself as a treat. If your market does not carry rabbit all the time, ask the butcher to special order it for you. Or, you can use 1 pound boneless, skinless chicken breast.

○ ○ ○

Bone the loins and the hind legs of the rabbit. The loins should yield about 5 ounces meat total, and the hind legs should yield about 11 ounces meat, for a total of 1 pound boneless meat.

In a sauté pan, melt 2 tablespoons of the butter over medium heat. Add the meat from the loins and legs and cook until the loins are lightly browned on both sides but not cooked through, 5 to 6 minutes. Transfer the loins to a plate. Continue to cook the legs for 3 to 5 minutes longer. You want to color the outside edges and firm the meat more. Set the rabbit meat aside to cool.

Fill a saucepan with water, bring to a boil, and salt lightly. Add the haricots verts and cook until tender-crisp, 2 to 3 minutes. Drain and refresh in a bowl filled with ice water. When cold, drain again and pat dry.

In a small bowl, whisk together the olive oil and 4 tablespoons of the vinegar, and then whisk in salt and pepper to taste to make a vinaigrette.

In another small bowl, whisk together the truffle paste, cream, 1 tablespoon of the vinegar, and a little salt.

cont'd

Insalata di coniglio con vinaigrette al tartufo
Rabbit Salad with Truffle Vinaigrette   cont'd

Cut the cooled rabbit pieces into ¼-inch-thick slices. Add the remaining 4 tablespoons butter to the sauté pan and place over low heat. When the butter melts, add the leg slices first and sauté for 5 minutes. Add the loin slices and sauté for 5 minutes longer. Season with salt and pepper and add the remaining 2 tablespoons vinegar. Stir well and add the tomato and chives. Cook very gently over low heat until the rabbit is cooked through and tender, about 5 minutes. Remove from the heat.

In a bowl, combine the haricots verts and mushrooms. Drizzle with three-fourths of the vinaigrette, sprinkle lightly with salt, and toss to coat evenly.

Arrange the watercress on a platter or 4 salad plates. Drizzle evenly with the remaining vinaigrette. Top with the warm rabbit slices and their pan juices, and drizzle the truffle dressing over the rabbit. Garnish the plate with the mushrooms and haricots verts.

Serve while the rabbit is warm.

SERVES 4

WINE: Go for a richly textured white wine, like a Ribolla or Fiano di Avellino. If you prefer a red, try a light Sangiovese from Emilia-Romagna (look for one from Tre Monti or Zerbina), or a Rosso Conero from Moroder, in the Marche.

Index

Antipasti Index

Antipasti

167 Index

Table of Equivalents

The exact equivalents in the following tables have been rounded for convenience.

Liquid/Dry Measures

U.S.	Metric
¼ teaspoon	1.25 milliliters
½ teaspoon	2.5 milliliters
1 teaspoon	5 milliliters
1 tablespoon (3 teaspoons)	15 milliliters
1 fluid ounce (2 tablespoons)	30 milliliters
¼ cup	60 milliliters
⅓ cup	80 milliliters
½ cup	120 milliliters
1 cup	240 milliliters
1 pint (2 cups)	480 milliliters
1 quart (4 cups, 32 ounces)	960 milliliters
1 gallon (4 quarts)	3.84 liters
1 ounce (by weight)	28 grams
1 pound	454 grams
2.2 pounds	1 kilogram

Length

U.S.	Metric
⅛ inch	3 millimeters
¼ inch	6 millimeters
½ inch	12 millimeters
1 inch	2.5 centimeters

Oven Temperature

Fahrenheit	Celsius	Gas
250	120	½
275	140	1
300	150	2
325	160	3
350	180	4
375	190	5
400	200	6
425	220	7
450	230	8
475	240	9
500	260	10